LIKE LOCKDOWN
NEVER HAPPENED

LIKE LOCKDOWN NEVER HAPPENED

MUSIC AND CULTURE DURING COVID

Joy White

Published by Repeater Books

An imprint of Watkins Media Ltd

Unit 11 Shepperton House

89-93 Shepperton Road

London

N1 3DF

United Kingdom

www.repeaterbooks.com

A Repeater Books paperback original 2024

1

Distributed in the United States by Random House, Inc., New York.

Copyright Joy White © 2024

Joy White asserts the moral right to be identified as the author of this work.

ISBN: 9781914420092

Ebook ISBN: 9781914420108

Printed and bound in the United Kingdom by CPI Group (UK) Ltd, Croydon, CR0 4YY

CONTENTS

INTRODUCTION/
INTERRUPTION

At the start of 2020, I was looking forward to the publication of my book *Terraformed* and eagerly anticipating a long-awaited holiday to Jamaica. Growing up Black in England means being out of place, so Jamaica is my place of belonging, where I saw, for the first time, older versions of myself. Over the last decade, life had taken a number of precarious and unexpected turns, so I had not visited for a while. Moving towards spring, like many of us I read reports of a virus that was spreading in China, but I did not fully take in what the impact of this would be. I carried on with my everyday routines with little awareness of what was to come.

One Monday in March 2020, I left work as usual. By Thursday, the process of lockdown had begun. Suddenly, everything moved online — work, play and family life. In many areas of the UK, in those early days, police patrolled the streets to make sure no one broke the new coronavirus laws and to enforce existing public order legislation. Children's playgrounds were locked up, and the rides were chained and put out of service. In the city, the streets were eerily quiet. In the UK, lockdown meant that we stayed at home. In those periods of deep isolation, technology allowed us to stay connected, but it also brought fear and death into our homes via daily and sometimes hourly updates on legacy and social media. We became more familiar with the workings of online meeting platform Zoom and the Houseparty app, while WhatsApp took on an even more significant role in sharing information and misinformation. We had to rethink what was meant by family, community, what it meant to be social. We were also forced to rethink how we consumed culture, music and entertainment.

Over the last few decades, advances in digital technology have made all forms of popular music more accessible. We can share, stream and download constantly. Exploring the ways in which we used music to pass the time during lockdown is a major strand of this book, and it is my attempt to make sense of chronological and "*kairotic*" time in that early era of the pandemic. While there is a broader socio-political picture — of revitalised Black Lives Matter protests in the aftermath of the murder of George Floyd, counter marches from the far-right, anti vax protests, anti-lockdown protests, demonstrations about police misuse of power — that is beyond the scope of this work, which will instead focus on the development in popular culture, and our consumption of it, during the pandemic.

Popular culture is founded on the everyday experiences, pleasures and interests of ordinary people. Watching drama and documentaries on television, listening to music and attending live music events are regular pastimes. And as Stuart Hall reminds us, "popular culture has become the dominant form of global culture".[1] It can be seen as a double movement of containment and resistance — keeping the masses entertained while at the same time offering an alternative site of cultural production as a counter narrative to the "high culture" of the ballet, the opera and the art gallery.

Black popular music is the focus of this book, and it is worth noting its reach beyond its immediate, everyday communities. Far from a monolith, it draws on Afrodiasporic influences and flows across cultural boundaries. While locating Black popular culture as a site of contradiction and contestation, Stuart Hall invites us to note that "in its rich production [...] and in its metaphorical use of the musical vocabulary, black popular culture has enabled the surfacing, of other forms of life".[2] In other words, Black popular culture makes Black life visible. Whatever form the cultural product may take — whether it's music, film, fashion or art — we are still able to see, in some way, Black life and Black experiences.

The consumption of popular Black music is not a trivial activity and, during a pandemic, takes on an even deeper significance. As Paul Gilroy points out, writing about album sleeves in the pre-internet era, these images, products and the processes of consumption "may express the need to belong, the desire to make blackness intelligible and somehow to fix that beauty and the pleasures it creates".[3] Stuart Hall reminds us that there is no essential Blackness. Black, as a category contains multitudes "immense diversity and differentiation of the historical and cultural experience of black subjects".[4] We therefore need a cultural lens that engages with that difference, so in this book I look at snapshots of online musical activity in the United States, South Africa, Jamaica and the United Kingdom. Writing in this moment about dancehall, lovers rock, rap, grime and UK drill as a soundtrack to pandemic time illustrates how the past and the present are "mediated and transformed by memory, fantasy and desire".[5] Black lives and Black creative expression are formed within a diasporic context, and that in itself complicates how musical sounds relate to the past and present moment.

What I have attempted to do in this book is to work through a nuanced critical analysis of Black music and its cultures. I have tried to develop a new way of thinking that operates on several scales, moving between "subnational, national and transnational methods and modes of enquiry".[6] To this end, I have taken into account Jamaica's musical significance as a cultural node, marking its artist contribution to the platform as well as its influence on the development of Black British music. While recognising the dominance of London, New York and Los Angeles in the global cultural economy, creative industries scholar Kim-Marie Spence points to Jamaica's significance and influence in Black musical expression, despite it being on the margins of the global.[7] In July 2022, I was finally able to travel to Jamaica. Originally planned for June 2020, my flight was delayed and then cancelled as the impact and consequences of Covid-19 became more apparent. In the years that had elapsed since my last visit, there had been many changes, including the rising popularity of afrobeats.[8] Once again, the main strip in Ocho Rios was the place to be. For peak season, though, it was quiet. Reliant on tourism as a major source of income, Jamaica had been hit hard by the global response to the pandemic and was only just getting back on its feet.

My starting point, therefore, is the global response to the pandemic, particularly in those first weeks and months. And while the data is important, it tells only one part of a complex, ongoing story. What we must also remember is how reliant we were on all forms of cultural, creative and digital content in this period. We passed the time on our own and with others. Music offered an important way to weather the pandemic, which for many of us was a unique situation. Widespread social restriction of this kind had not happened in living memory in the UK. An interrogation of the political and economic landscape during pandemic time provides details of some aspects of the effect of Covid-19: job losses, changes to working patterns and so on. However, as popular culture is one of the ways that we give our lives meaning, it provides another equally important dimension.

In the pandemic era that is the focus of this book — March 2020–December 2021, including those periods of "lockdown" or restricted life — time stood still in many ways, but it also shifted and changed shape. As we travelled through time and space while staying still, the context of home shifted. Three years on from lockdown, isolation and social restriction, we have been encouraged to go back to work, but what we return to cannot be the same,[9] even if the hand sanitiser stations are less prominent now. During lockdown, we shared our lives online in different time zones, experiencing an intergenerational, planetary enjoyment of musical forms and formats. Geographical and sonic borders became blurred, porous and fuzzy.

As Black creative expression is so fundamental to how many of us passed the time during this period, this book uses the concepts of Black joy and sonic Black geographies to explore what Christopher Small calls *"musicking"*. Musicking involves dancing, playing, listening to, as well as making music, and I have extended the concept for our digital age to include responding to and commenting on music. I look at Black creative expression as it is formed and shared in the crucible of the pandemic. In the pandemic, the usual markers of time disappeared, and the tempo of life shifted dramatically. By December 2020, as vaccines became available, governments started to make plans for coming out of lockdown. When the world started to open up again in the summer of 2021, street signs appeared giving instructions on where to stand and how to keep our distance. Our "musicking" activities in this period became more measured and less spontaneous.

The Black Atlantic flow of musical expression is at the heart of this book. Black musical forms — including dancehall, lovers rock, rap, grime and UK drill — are discussed here not only as sites of cultural resistance but also as spaces of Black joy, as well as modes of belonging. During the pandemic, Black musical expression offered a way for people to articulate changes in material conditions and counter the effects of social isolation. What we cannot escape, though, is the logic of neoliberalism, where individual success and triumphs are highlighted more than institutional and structural inequalities, even in pandemic time. Bearing this in mind, it is possible to see how, as Paul Gilroy asserts, music's "traditional concern" with "love, care, loss, death and inevitable suffering" has taken a backseat to "playful iteration of stereotypes, bragging and personal brand-building".[10] Taking this into account, I have carefully considered the ways in which rap, grime and UK drill articulate social commentary and a sense of place, as well as a politics of belonging.[11]

Under neoliberalism, formed as part of the neoliberal project that displaced the consensus politics of the 1950s and 1960s, the economy relies on market forces to provide goods and services, and so "enterprise culture" becomes embedded in our contemporary social moment. Even in pandemic time, entrepreneurship continued to be seen as common sense. Governments that centre market forces and enterprise culture give rise to a society where public services are outsourced, the welfare state is rolled back, and lower wages and the worsening of working conditions are commonplace. Issues that previously fell within a societal remit have increasingly become the responsibility of individuals, and people are seen as having a "moral duty to take care of themselves."[12] A focus on individual responsibility is complicated, however, by the need during the pandemic to work together as a community.

Enterprise culture includes music as a commodity, and musicians are compelled to embody an entrepreneurial spirit as part of their everyday practice if they want to survive. It is also worth saying that, prior to lockdown, many musicians were already experiencing a precarious existence, working for very little and combining various income streams. Nevertheless, innovative responses during pandemic time by organisations and individual musicians meant that music could still be made and shared.

The focus of this book is the conjuncture of globalisation, contemporary Black musical expression and passing time in a pandemic. The backdrop, in the UK at least, is more than a decade of austerity, catastrophic capitalism, widening inequalities and a hollowed-out social infrastructure. Over five chapters, I explore the ways in which online "imagined communities"[13] formed through contemporary Black musical expression sustained us in pandemic time. Through an eclectic selection of popular sonic events — including the viral #DontRushChallenge, Swizz Beatz and Timbaland's online *Verzuz* battles, musical releases from Ghetts, Kano, Dave, TeeZandos and Headie One, as well as the emergence of No Signal online radio — I contextualise and illustrate how Black popular culture helped people to pass time in a unique situation.

CHAPTER 1
A WINDOW IN TIME

Stay at Home, Protect the NHS, Save Lives[1]

... it's going to spread further and I must level with you, level with the British public, many more families are going to lose loved ones before their time.
UK Prime Minister Boris Johnson, 12 March 2020[2]

Across the world, government actions to mitigate against Covid-19 heralded an extraordinary interruption to routine and everyday life. For this opening chapter, I have selected a window in time — from March 2020 to December 2021 — when the most severe restrictions were in place. During those early days, weeks and months, the world woke up not just to the enormity of what was at stake but also to the enduring socio-economic consequences of the pandemic. The UK was badly affected by Covid-19, and the quote above from Boris Johnson signals the "hands-off", "some-people-are-dispensable" approach that shaped UK government response in those early days. The terrible consequences of Covid-19 in the UK clearly illustrated the effects of a hollowed-out public infrastructure, the eradication of welfare services and entrenched inequality.

Cast your mind back to the early weeks of 2020, as stories about a new virus began to appear via news sites and online.

On 30 January 2020, the World Health Organization (WHO) declared Covid-19 a novel coronavirus, stating that it constituted a public health emergency of international concern (PHIC).[3] In February 2020, the *British Medical Journal* (*BMJ*) reported that in Italy confirmed cases "leapt by 45% to reach 322".[4] By March, we were seeing regular images of Italian citizens singing from their balconies. Italy was the first EU country to confine people to their homes, when, in an effort to contain the spread of the virus, the whole population was placed under quarantine.[5] In other parts of Europe, lockdown took on various modes: in France, activities were permitted but only upon completion of a form, and people were only allowed out alone and could not go more than one kilometre from home; Spain had an extended national lockdown and banned outdoor physical exercise. Most EU nations closed borders and restricted travel in some way.[6]

As more news emerged, we began to understand the significance of the first wave of Covid-19, first revealed in December 2019 as coming from Wuhan, mainland China. The first known death was reported on 11 January 2020.[7] Gradually extending to other countries, measures were imposed to try to halt the spread of the virus.[8] On 11 March 2020, the World Health Organization declared that Covid-19 was a global pandemic. Although there have been several pandemics since the 1980s — including Human Immunodeficiency Virus (HIV) (1981), Severe Acute Respiratory Syndrome Coronavirus (SARS-CoV) (2002), Middle East Respiratory Syndrome Coronavirus (MERS-CoV) (2012), Ebola virus (2013)[9] — none have had such major consequences for the global economy as Covid-19.

An early focus group study carried out before the implementation of the vaccine showed how the Covid-19 pandemic presented a considerable challenge to global public health.[10] In the UK, government responses at that time — prior to the vaccine becoming available — relied on non-pharmaceutical interventions (regular, thorough handwashing, social distancing and social isolation). Other non-pharmaceutical interventions included the banning of public gatherings and the closure of schools, all non-essential shops, workplaces and services, coupled with a recommendation to keep a distance of at least two metres apart. In anticipation of a potential lockdown, panic-buying of bottled water, pasta and toilet paper was reported with mounting hysteria.[11] Photographs of empty supermarket shelves shared on social media added to a sense of scarcity and shortage, and shoppers were urged to be considerate and "not stockpile food".[12]

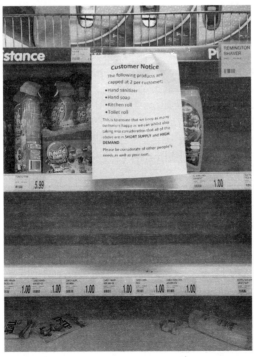

Supermarket rationing notice, March 2020

Covid-19: A Global Overview

Although the world got the notification about Covid-19 at the same time, the response to the announcement differed. Some countries — such as Australia, New Zealand, Vietnam and China — immediately put comprehensive measures in place; others, including the USA and the UK, adopted a more cautious approach. As a result, the difference in consequences for each country and region were considerable. The numbers of people contracting Covid-19, as well as the deaths from it, were highest in the USA and the UK. The UK was particularly badly affected by Covid-19, with the highest number of deaths in Europe.[13] The data below compares deaths per million in the UK against other countries in the Global North:

Australia: total cases 7,920; total deaths 104; total population approximately 25 million; total cases/million 317; total deaths/million 4.

New Zealand: total cases 1,528; total deaths 22; total population approximately 5 million; total cases/million 306; total deaths/million 4.

USA: total cases 2,849,111; total deaths 132,200; total population approximately 333 million; total cases/million 8,556; total deaths/million 397.

Canada: total cases 104,271; total deaths 8,615; total population approximately 38 million; total cases 2,744; total deaths/million 227.

UK: total cases 283,372; total deaths 40,553; total population approximately 68 million; total cases/million 4,167; total deaths/million 596.[14]

Given the more fragile health and social care infrastructure on the African continent, the incidence and death rate from Covid-19 was low compared to better-off countries in the Global North. Although this may be due to limited testing, it also appears that a younger population, as well as prior experience with previous pandemics — for example, Ebola,[15] smallpox, HIV and malaria[16] — enhanced preparedness to tackle Covid-19. Over the whole continent of 1.2 billion people, there were 140 million cases and three million deaths. Nevertheless, the economic impact in terms of loss of income and food insecurity will be significant.[17]

A number of political, social, economic and cultural factors affected how different global regions initially reacted to the pandemic. In the early months, February to July 2020, the responses varied widely, and there are many reasons for this. But in the main, it came down to healthcare, available financial resources, whether the population trusted the government, what type of economic support was provided and whether people trusted that support. Cultural factors (such as high levels of individualism) were also a significant determinant in how different populations reacted to the pandemic restrictions, and whether people complied with these measures depended on how individualistic people were, and whether they valued their individual needs more or less than those of the wider society.[18]

In Western Europe, the first wave of the virus had devastating consequences. Western European countries were slow to take the pandemic seriously, with early efforts mostly focused on giving overseas aid rather than reviewing and consolidating their own pandemic responses, such as the sending of shipments of personal protective equipment (PPE) to China during January to March 2020, while the virus was spreading across Europe. A combination of slow responses, timewasting on disagreements regarding how the virus was spread, the efficacy of handwashing, whether masks should be compulsory and, in light of all these unknowns and uncertainty, the appropriate level of PPE for healthcare workers — these are all factors in explaining why in Western Europe and North America the first waves of Covid-19 were particularly disastrous.[19]

As the focus of this book is the Black Atlantic flow and exchange of contemporary music during the pandemic, it is useful to take a moment to consider Jamaica's response, particularly as it relies heavily on tourism. Although it is a small island, Jamaica also wields significant cultural influence through music.[20] By implementing measures in the early days of the pandemic, it appeared to be managing well, with a small number of infections and deaths.[21] Researcher Lisa Vasciannie also outlines how the Jamaican government, mindful of its reliance on tourist income, responded to the pandemic as a serious threat. Public services were closed or suspended, as were schools and universities. As a result, entertainment and tourism were severely restricted.[22]

The question remains as to why the UK was so badly affected by Covid-19, particularly when, by many measures, it is more economically developed than West Africa or the Caribbean, for example. According to the data, there were 596 total deaths per million as well as a substantial economic downturn.[23] We have to view the impact of Covid-19 in the UK within the context of an established infrastructure that includes a National Health Service (albeit stretched and underfunded), which offers healthcare that is mostly free at the point of delivery; where there is accessible, clean water (again with the caveat that there is shit in the sea) and access to quality food (as long as you can pay). However, if we take into account more than a decade of austerity, a populist government and stresses on the economy and instability caused by Brexit, then it is possible to see why the impact was so terrible.[24] Added to this is that the UK government's initial response was one of minimal intervention (and the hope for "herd immunity"), compounded by slow actions, confused guidance and quarantine policies that were less than rigorous.[25] In December 2020, the prime minister announced tighter social restrictions; non-essential shops were closed and households in London and the South East were told not to mix. In yet another U-turn, families were then advised that only up to three households could gather on Christmas Day.[26]

Street sign, social distancing, November 2020

Covid-19: A UK Context

Looking at a timeline of events in the UK provides the context for this chapter, starting on 16 March 2020 with an announcement from Prime Minister Boris Johnson, and ending on 15 December 2021.[27] In early March 2020, the government allowed schools, shops, restaurants and workplaces to remain open. Although the government imposed light border restrictions, large public events were allowed to take place. On 13 March, the Cheltenham Festival — a four-day horse racing event with around sixty thousand people each day — was allowed to go ahead. After the festival, there appeared to be a significant local spike in Covid-19 deaths and cases.[28] Subsequent UK government responses to the pandemic included a number of public health measures, including lockdowns, the temporary closure of non-essential businesses, social distancing, social restriction and eventually quarantine for travellers. People had their lives restricted in a number of far-reaching ways.

Initially, the UK government adopted a policy of herd immunity. However, after criticism from the WHO, the government changed their approach. From 23 March 2020, the first lockdown measures were put in place — all leisure facilities, pubs, restaurants and non-essential shops were closed, and a wage replacement or furlough scheme for non-essential workers was put in place. People were asked to work from home if possible, unless they were essential key workers such as bus drivers, delivery drivers, NHS staff and carers for elderly, disabled and vulnerable people. On 25 March 2020, a key piece of legislation, the Coronavirus Act 2020, came into force, and emergency powers were introduced to make people comply with the measures to stop the spread of the virus. By 18 July, local authorities in England were given additional powers to enforce social distancing.

By the end of March 2020, in preparation for and anticipation of many Covid-19-related deaths, extra mortuary facilities appeared in a number of locations, including Wanstead Flats in East London.[29] By January 2021, further facilities were opened at Breakspear Crematorium in Ruislip, Leatherhead and RAF Coltishall in Norwich.[30] So-called "Nightingale Hospitals" were built on several sites, but insufficient staff were supplied to work in them. These hospitals opened with great fanfare but were poorly used. So few patients were treated that by May 2020 all of them were "placed on standby".[31] Many of these sites were repurposed as mass vaccination or testing centres.[32] In general, hospitals reported a lack of PPE — the images of singing Italians on balconies were soon replaced with those of hard-pressed NHS workers bruised by inadequate equipment and exhausted from long shifts.

Social mixing was severely restricted, with people confined to their households and contact limited to close family members. Exercise was permitted for one hour each day. Lockdown measures were enforced by law, with fines issued for those breaking the rules. Parks were closed, which presented a significant challenge in poor inner-city areas with little outside space. In many areas, police patrolled the streets to ensure that rules were being adhered to, adding an increased layer of potential for conflict, and possible over-policing of particular communities. Some celebrities fell afoul of the law — singer Rita Ora was fined £10,000 for having a birthday party[33] — and there were other high-profile incidents relating to people gathering in large groups to socialise. In June 2020, more than five hundred revellers attended an outdoor block party in Harlesden.[34] While in Birmingham, police put a stop to an unlicensed street party attended by approximately seventy people.[35]

As Covid-19 cases rose, a second lockdown period began on 5 November 2020 and ran for a few more weeks — ending on 26 November when local restrictions were put in place instead.[36] By December 2020, the first vaccine was administered, followed by a mass vaccination programme. A modified tiered system was then reintroduced throughout most of the country, as a step on the way to opening up. Nevertheless, by the start of the following year, a third national lockdown occurred due to a new Covid-19 variant. From 6 January 2021, restrictions were imposed as in the first, but this time people could form "support bubbles".[37] By 8 March 2021, England initiated a phased exit from lockdown and the government published a roadmap out of lockdown to ease and then lift restrictions for the whole country.[38] At the time of writing, the long-term socio-economic impact of Covid-19 is ongoing.

Socio-Economic Impact of Covid-19 in the UK

Across the globe, governments including the UK put in place a range of policy measures in an attempt to mitigate some of the worst health, social and economic implications: social distancing, wearing masks in public places, restrictions on travel (local, national and international), closing borders, urging (and sometimes mandating) residents to stay at home, as well as limitations on the size of social gatherings.[39] Those restrictions dramatically affected the tourism and hospitality industry; sectors already impacted by "low profit margins and vulnerability to external shocks" were dramatically affected by these measures.[40]

Businesses had to adapt quickly to provide other ways to deliver goods and services, utilising social distancing measures and, where possible, shifting to online delivery. However, for some businesses, such as airlines and airports, the only solution was to stop altogether. By early

2020, the Covid-19 outbreak and subsequent pandemic had resulted in over 4.3 million confirmed cases and over 290,000 deaths globally.[41] It has also sparked fears of an impending economic crisis and recession. Social distancing, self-isolation and travel restrictions have led to a reduced workforce across all economic sectors and caused many jobs to be lost. After the World Health Organization declared the Covid-19 outbreak as a global emergency in January 2020,[42] some of the world's largest economies attempted to "flatten the curve" by enforcing reductions on movement and border shutdowns.

Despite an initial approach of minimal intervention, the fear of economic doom forced the UK government to act. On 20 March, Chancellor Rishi Sunak announced a £330 billion package of emergency loan guarantees to help businesses that were facing financial difficulty. Other interventions included a Covid-19 job retention scheme[43]; deferred VAT and income tax payments; statutory sick pay relief package for SMEs; a twelve-month business works holiday for all retail, hospitality, leisure and nursery businesses in England; a small business grant funding of £10,000 for all business in receipt of small business rate relief or rural rate relief; and grant funding of £25,000 for retail, hospitality and leisure businesses with a low property rateable value. The Coronavirus Business Interruption Loan Scheme offered loans of up to £5 million for SMEs from the Bank of England to support liquidity among larger firms, helping them to bridge disruption to their cash flow.[44]

The first lockdown period was sudden and wide-ranging — people were faced with isolation and a lack of face-to-face contact. The UK government had to strike a balance between containing the virus and the social, economic and psychological impact of restrictive measures. As well as being expected to adhere to social isolation guidelines, there were further restrictions for those showing symptoms or testing positive — including quarantine periods of seven and fourteen days. One of the many consequences of lockdown was social isolation. Noting the effect on different communities, scholars in one study identified a theme of loss: loss of income, structure and routine; loss of motivation and loss of self-worth.[45]

During the early days of the pandemic, to "protect the NHS" older people were discharged from hospital into care homes. Matt Hancock (then Secretary of State for Health and Social Care) assured the public that there would be a "protective ring" around residential care homes. However, this was not the case — as well as high rates of hospitalisation, older people had much higher death rates in general, particularly those in residential care homes.[46] As the first restrictions were put in place, from March 2020, adults over the age of seventy were required to self-isolate. This meant staying at home for three months to reduce the risk of infection. Concerns regarding wellbeing for this social group are well documented. However, when certain factors were in place, the adverse psychosocial effects of lockdown could be mitigated by offers of support from social contacts, a stable living environment, cohabiting with others and financial security. In addition, older adults could draw on their past lived experience to make sense of what was in many ways a unique situation.[47] The same was not true of young people.

The Impact of Covid-19 on Young People

Although the damaging effects of lockdown were significant across the general population, for young people, the effect was more acute and long-lasting even after restrictions were lifted. Research carried out during and between the lockdown periods showed the adverse psychological impact of Covid-19 on young people in the UK.[48] Researchers interviewed adolescents and young adults about their experiences during the Covid-19 pandemic. Social isolation and restricted mobility meant that in-person contact was limited. The closure of schools and universities disrupted education and meant no access to the aligned support services. Many children were away from school and usual leisure activities for six months during the first lockdown.[49]

For those young people from ethnic minority communities, or who had pre-existing mental health conditions, the effect of lockdown on mental health was even more intense.[50] During the early lockdowns, the prevailing view was that children and young people were less likely to become physically ill or require hospitalisation, and therefore less attention was paid to the effects of isolation and social distancing on mental health. However, what researchers found was that "emerging evidence suggests that young people have experienced the greatest decline in mental health in the first wave of Covid-19 in comparison to people in other age ranges".[51]

Moving from adolescence to young adulthood can be a challenging time, as young people experience major life transitions. The disruption wrought by Covid-19 restrictions on young people's everyday lives was significant. Adding to the uncertainty was a daily roll call of death and infection.[52] Compounded by a shift to online learning, and its adjacent anxieties around digital access and having a quiet place to work, these anxieties were keenly felt by those from low-income homes. It is evident from the data collected that even though other population groups felt the effects of isolation and lack of restricted mobility, for young people the effects were even more damaging. And for young people who were from marginalised backgrounds, they were even more so.

An analysis of social distancing restrictions showed how

it affected social lives, mental health and wellbeing. The study highlights key points such as feeling lonely, missing social contact, particularly at the start of lockdown, frustration at missing out on major life events and also notes that even though they could socialise online, many chose not increase their time online. Some were overwhelmed by feelings of being trapped at home, unable to escape and unable to take part in their usual activities.[53] The initial lockdown period had no tangible endpoint, as it kept getting pushed back. Even when lockdown eased, the requirement to social distance and wear masks in public places meant that social contact was still restricted.

As researchers in this area remind us, disruptions to education on this scale had not occurred since the Second World War.[54] These changes are likely to have long-term consequences requiring ongoing support, with particular attention needed on how socio-demographic factors affected young people's experiences during the pandemic. Around 60% of students living in affluent areas had access to online learning during the pandemic compared with 23% of students in more deprived areas.[55] The long-term effects of school closures on young people's health, income and productivity are yet to be fully realised.

The UK was one of the nations most affected by Covid-19, with a large number of cases, as well as a high number of deaths. Combined with the subsequent economic downturn, children and young people were severely impacted by events that they had no input into or control over. UK children lived through one of the most long-lasting lockdowns globally. Many were away from school for up to six months in the first lockdown, and during the third lockdown schools were closed for an indefinite period. Children and young people experienced all of the social and economic collateral impacts of Covid-19, including the economic downturn with associated job losses for parents and carers, as well as the resulting negative impact on wellbeing.[56]

In a society that was already deeply unequal, the effects of lockdown intensified this inequality, reinforcing and exacerbating existing divides. People from ethnic minorities and low-income communities were disproportionately fined for breaking lockdown[57] and less likely to have access to green space in which to undertake their daily exercise safely. Morbidity and mortality rates were the highest in the most deprived neighbourhoods, among the very old and among most Black and ethnic minority communities.[58] Almost a year after the first lockdown, it became more evident that those in poorer communities were being disproportionately affected.[59]

The Impact on the Music Industry

As the focus of this book is popular music, I now turn to the impact of Covid-19 on the music industry, where it evidently caused major disruption on a global scale. Yet at the same time, consumers had an even greater need for ways to keep themselves entertained and occupied while they were at home (although for some, who were deemed to be essential or key workers, work continued in the same format, albeit with the weight of a potentially deadly virus in the background). Online activity therefore took on a new significance for all age groups and across all communities.

During this period, live events in the creative and cultural industries ground to a halt. Live events are a mainstay of the UK music sector — millions of "music tourists" travel to the UK every year from all over Europe to attend concerts and festivals.[60] The music industry was ravaged not only by the social restrictions during the first wave of the pandemic, but also by the consequences of

Brexit,[61] as festivals and events were postponed and then cancelled. SXSW was one of the first major festivals to be cancelled in 2020, followed by Glastonbury, as all other live events planned for the summer of 2020 came to a sudden halt.[62] This meant that musicians had to adapt the way that they shared their music, with many switching to livestreaming, using social media such as Instagram to connect with their fans.

The UK popular music industry is a billion-pound affair — as well as contributing £5.2 billion to the UK economy, it also forms a significant part of the wider global economy. As a key component of the creative and cultural industries, music is deeply significant.[63] From the outset there was a real concern that the music industry would not survive lockdown, as its self-employed and freelance workers were initially not included in the bounce-back measures introduced by the chancellor.[64]

A study of online entertainment during the pandemic evaluated the impact of Covid-19 on the creative and cultural industries, including music and live events.[65] The study's overall finding was that the impact of the Covid-19 restrictions was severe, with major economic loss and disruption. It also found that mental health problems associated with lockdown had negatively affected the creativity, productivity and mood of music industry makers. As performances moved online, festivals became more inclusive events and online streaming became the new normal for the music industry.[66] The numbers of people participating in online events increased, and there were a number of formats at work, such live sessions on social media or sharing a pre-recorded event. In this way, musical performance became much more accessible. It should also be noted that musicians in inherently DIY genres such as grime or drill already had existing reach and platforms in place.[67] There is an ongoing question, however, regarding the long-term impact of the cancellation and postponement of live events.

Despite the loss of jobs and income, as well as lockdown restrictions and closed venues, some young musicians actually valued the additional time that they had to make and listen to music. At the same time, there was increased pressure on young people and the longer-term adverse impacts pointed to economic instability and unemployment for years to come. Effectively, these short-term gains were at the expense of long-term aspirations.[68]

Industries in every sector were affected by the pandemic; however, the creative and cultural industries, hospitality and tourism were especially hard hit.[69] According to the UK Music's annual report, "more than a third of UK music industry workers lost jobs", and the value of British music overseas "slumped by 23%".[70] Cancelled festivals and events that could not be rescheduled led to even more uncertainty and job losses in a sector that was already precarious for many. By January 2021, music festivals had experienced a 90% fall in revenue. According to the Association of Independent Festivals, one in six festivals permanently closed during or just after Covid-19. In response, UK Music put together a detailed six-point action plan for support.[71] However, it was not until August 2021 that a government insurance for live events and festivals was put in place,[72] almost a year after a similar scheme was introduced for film and TV production.[73]

Conclusion

From March 2020 to December 2021, the Covid-19 pandemic changed the way that we lived, worked and entertained ourselves. Its ramifications are wide-ranging and ongoing. Anxiety and fear, as well as economic stress, still linger as a result of the pandemic and its associated restrictions. Some of the consequences have been outlined here, but as the pandemic is not yet over, it is a moving picture. In those early days, the UK response was cautious, hesitant and motivated by a reluctance of those in power to accept the severity of the situation. As the days, weeks and months wore on, we saw the politicians who were supposed to protect us and make decisions for the public good treat a deadly situation as an opportunity to build power and resources. More than a decade of austerity had already left public institutions ill-prepared to coordinate a meaningful response. Instead, contracts to provide essential services such as PPE were doled out to the private sector, often with little oversight. As a result, the UK ended up with the highest cases and death rate in Europe.

I find it difficult to think and write about this time without feeling overwhelmed by the sheer depth and scale of what we went through. So, as I often do, I turn to popular music as a way to make sense of this unique experience. What is clear is that during the period that is the focus for this book, there was a shift in how we participated in music, using it to stay connected and to manage the isolation that came with lockdown. As we were isolated and then socially distanced, time changed shape. How we look back on pandemic time, while in this present moment, is explored in the remaining chapters.

CHAPTER 2
PLAYING WITH TIME —
CHRONOS AND KAIROS

In pandemic time, time felt as though it stood still. In other moments, it changed shape, encompassing long periods without the usual, expected markers that let us know we are moving from one phase to the next. From March 2020 to December 2021, many of us were in isolation and were passing time through the screen, on our phones, on computers and on television. On these screens, we saw our faces reflected back at us as meetings and other interactions moved online. After the first couple of weeks, as the days rolled on, what at first seemed like an extended holiday gradually became a routine with no end in sight. I was added to one of many new WhatsApp groups where we adopted strategies and tried out activities to pass the time. Our "quarantine group" alleviated the monotonous nature of those early days. Family members from London, the Midlands and the South East took part in virtual running sessions on Fridays, a cooking challenge, a bake-off event (I had never baked a cake before lockdown, so my deconstructed banoffee tart brought chaos and confusion), as well as endless quizzes and games. The group became a place for general news and updates, and at its peak there were up to fifteen people posting daily content. I connected with some family members more frequently than I had in previous years. Existing WhatsApp groups, supplemented by Zoom meetings and catch ups on the Houseparty app, also cleared a path through the daily predictability and isolation. Every so often, an unidentified voice note would land, one which had been "forwarded many times" that gave "secret insider information" on the government's plan for military rule. Passing the time meant finding ways to blunt our senses and to mitigate feelings of boredom and fear.

We found different ways to entertain ourselves, to keep our minds occupied and to keep track of time. In everyday time, music and sound can create a locus of individual comfort as well as offer a sense of connection with a wider community. During the lockdown period, music allowed an escape from boredom and isolation.[1] Music flowed between us in various forms, contexts and formats — online and via broadcast — as we tried to make sense of how life had changed. As a cultural resource, music offered a way to reflect on self-identity, as well as a way to work through changing emotional states. As lockdown extended through hours and days into weeks, music formed part of the care of the self, helping people to shift mood or energy levels,[2] while staying at home to "save lives and protect the NHS".

For key workers such as nurses, doctors, delivery drivers, care workers and cleaners, the clock continued to mark time in its customary fashion, as these maintained a consistent pattern of employment (albeit with a deadly virus in the air). At the start of the first lockdown in March 2020, children were still at school, and lessons carried on, routinely segmented by the clock. Even though the rhythms of the day continued, space and place looked and felt different, encompassing altered tempos and offbeat sounds. At work, my university time became divided into synchronous and asynchronous tasks. Teaching moved online, and I engaged with disembodied voices as I heard, but rarely saw, groups of people who were trying their best to maintain some kind of student identity.

A Meditation on Time

How we remember or document the history of that time (especially as it is still unfolding) requires something more than a linear narrative.[3] However, in this contemporary historical moment, it is not really possible to take a step back because the view from a distance is not that far away. In ordinary time, we may go through life on autopilot, not really paying much attention to the minutiae of life. In pandemic time, through necessity, life is brought into much sharper focus. What I am attempting to do here is document some aspects of that contemporary conjuncture using sequential, quantitative time (*chronos*) as well as fluctuating, qualitative time (*kairos*).

So how to meditate on time when it is sequential, fluctuating and during a pandemic? Philosopher Michael Marder has a useful concept, "passenger time" — a sense of time that allows us to consider how we can mark the span between places, as well as take into account our departure and our destination. Although the clock keeps us in sequential time, how we experience it is particular to us. Passenger time is situated within an organising frame of "passengerhood", defined as the "perceived and measurable duration in passage in between places and in between times". It is not about the end goal, but more about what happens in between.[4]

How we experience time depends on mood — it can drag; it can go fast (time flies). But whatever its speed, time passes. For millennia "human mobility has structured our thinking of time".[5] Moving through, within and around distinct locations allows us to signpost and measure what has passed. So, what happens to and with time if you have to stay in place (stay at home, save lives)? I have indicated the role of music in marking time throughout lockdown and I will address that in more detail later in this chapter. However, there were other fleeting, sonic events that helped to mark time too. On Thursdays at 8pm, over a ten-week period, we clapped for the NHS.[6] Across the UK, during a period when most activities had to take place in isolation, people moved to their doorsteps, balconies and windows to participate in mass community applause.

Clapping/applause can symbolise a number of things: in music it can provide the beat for a song or a dance; outside of music it can show approval or — as a slow hand clap — disapproval. Applause takes place in space and time, how long the clapping lasts for might signify the depth of the approval.[7] From my doorstep, for the first four weeks of lockdown, I recorded the sound of the applause. As the event progressed, other sounds were incorporated, including cheers, the beat of saucepan lids and, in my neighbourhood, the guy from corner shop blowing his trumpet for the NHS. Over time, though, the event became divisive for a number of reasons. All of the sounds, applause, cheers and trumpets gradually became more muted until eventually it stopped entirely.

Pandemic time brought in a raft of restrictions, including lockdown, quarantine and social distancing. It was sudden, and even though news reports signposted what was happening elsewhere, the duration kept shifting. Almost overnight, our ability to travel from one destination to another was curtailed. At the same time, isolation meant that in some instances even moving from room to room was limited if a household member had tested positive. Increasingly, how we thought about travel and made sense of everyday pursuits, such as keeping ourselves entertained, became more urgent. Whether we were passing the time or making time, technology allowed us to make, share and record memories and experiences while confined to our homes.[8]

Black Kairos: Online Black Identities

As more of us moved online as part of our everyday practice, Black communities became more visible in these spaces. In *Digital Diaspora*, Anna Everett writes that afro-diasporic communities are early adopters of new media forms,[9] using these technologies to create and share content. Black digital practice in this context can be understood in a multitude of ways as a place to share and define cultural identity, to make connection and seek community, a place for healing as well as pleasure. Black life online allows for a richer existence that goes beyond contours defined for us in the everyday.[10] As media scholar André Brock Jr notes, in the last few years, "Black digital practice has become very much a mainstream phenomenon",[11] as — often unacknowledged — sounds, visuals and words become embedded in an everyday lexicon.

If Black creativity and Black cultural aesthetics (via the internet) are already hyper-visible, then this was heightened by pandemic time, when more of us were online and for longer periods. Thinking with and through fluctuating, qualitative time, Brock invites us to consider the concept of "Black Kairos" as racial performance (in person or digital), intervention or timely engagement within a "communicative and cultural context".[12] "Black Kairos" also attends to the political and economic lens, and seeks to understand digital activity through "commodification, capacity for surveillance and economic potential".[13] Brock reminds us that "the temporality of Black Kairos is apparent in the riposte and swagger of face-to-face interactions, but historically, it has been much less visible in ICTs".[14] The internet and social media have allowed a larger number of participants to "create their own discourse styles and mechanisms".[15] The #DontRushChallenge, which I explore later in this chapter, illustrates the ways in which a Black cultural aesthetic went viral online in pandemic time.

Online, the hashtag and the algorithm make it plain that as well as being hyper-visible, Black life online is social, inviting comments, contributions and care across geographical and generational lines. It is a place that reminds us that Black life is not solely defined by racism, violence, trauma and grief. Black expression flows across the digital landscape, connecting afro-diasporic communities as they participate in cyberspace. What the internet has done is placed us in intergenerational spaces that are less compartmentalised than life offline.

Rap on the Internet: #DontRush...

Globally, rap is one of the most popular musical forms. As a product of the Black Atlantic world, rap flows beyond national borders, crossing boundaries and changing shape. As Tricia Rose writes, rap, in all its forms, often voices the struggles and successes of marginalised communities.[16]

Rap is socially constructed as a medium of violence both lyrically and visually. As a Black art form that speaks to Black audiences and the wider community simultaneously, rap resonates with the marginalised and the disadvantaged around the globe. Rap has a considerable digital presence, and many people come to experience it via the internet and through social media. For geographically diverse communities, the internet becomes the main entry point. While artists might make music that is located in specific places, these geographical origins are transcended when the work is mediated online.[17] During the pandemic, when life was restricted in so many ways, Black digital culture, including rap, formed the foundation for dance crazes, memes and challenges, mediated in and through online contexts.

In April 2020, in the early days of lockdown, the #DontRushChallenge became a viral sensation on TikTok. In approximately two weeks, over seventy-nine thousand videos with the hashtag #DontRushChallenge were created, in which people recorded themselves in leisure wear or pyjamas and then transformed into a more glamourous version of themselves. The featured soundtrack was "Don't Rush" by Young T & Bugsey (Ra'chard Tucker and Doyin Julius), a Nottingham-based rap duo. Eventually, a range of others joined in, including the cast of *Orange is the New Black*,[18] doctors in the UK and in US,[19] Turkish cabin crew[20] and the US military,[21] as well as women from South Africa, Yemen and Ghana.[22] An official compilation video was released in May 2020.[23] "Don't Rush" was then remixed to feature North London rapper Headie One in May 2020.[24] Another two remixes followed: one in May, featuring Latin-R&B and dancehall artist Rauw Alejandro[25]; and one in June, featuring American rapper DaBaby.[26] Globalisation and accessible technology inform the flow of communication or "digital dialogue" between people and communities in different locations. Widespread participation and engagement with the #DontRushChallenge illustrates how Black creative expression connected people online.

What is less well-known is that this globally successful music challenge was initiated by a group of Black girls — students at the University of Hull— who just wanted something to do to pass the time during lockdown.[27] Writing when the challenge was in its third week, journalist Antoinette Isama stated, "Black women effortlessly celebrate their diverse cultures, professions, and interests all in short clips". In an interview with *Teen Vogue* in April 2020, one of the initiators of the challenge, Toluwalase Asolo, a twenty-year-old business management student, explained how the group started the challenge as a response to boredom. As they had to keep social distance in their student accommodation, video footage was shared initially via WhatsApp.[28]

During the various lockdown periods, people missed out on everyday, in-person interactions. In the city, where individuals are rooted in a culture of noise, the streets emptied and became much quieter, there was far less sound in the air. This change was challenging.[29] Social restriction and social isolation caused a psychic shift in how we lived together (or apart). Crucially, what emerges from this unprecedented era are the ways in which we passed the time (kairos), the global significance of Black online presence and how we utilised our technologies of the self during lockdown.

Finding ways to pass the time when life was severely restricted in a multitude of ways was extremely arduous. In 2020, during the early months of the pandemic — namely March, April and May — chronological time was marked by the many online performances of the #DontRushChallenge. In the numerous responses to the challenge we see online, in passenger time, participants transformed themselves for a night out that is not going to happen. In kairotic time, people found joy, pleasure and community in a group activity — even if they could not physically be in the same place. Videos were recorded separately at a distance and then spliced together and shared. The #DontRushChallenge is a sonic event that speaks to the confluence of people and place in Britain's multicultural present, as the heritage of the originators of the challenge includes young women of Congolese, Nigerian, Sierra Leonean and Turks and Caicos descent.

Black Online Presence: The Global Importance of Black Digital Practice

Black online identities and Black digital practice therefore take on an increased significance in pandemic time. Using André Brock's framework of Critical Technocultural Discourse Analysis (CTDA), we can see in the responses to the challenge how cultural identity is filtered online, and that for Black participants it was a place to use their own voice and define themselves in non-reductive ways. Stepping into the digital space allowed for movement outside of stereotypical racialised categories.[30] How technology is used depends, to some extent, on cultural identities, and as digital media scholar Francesca Sobande reminds us, "Black people across the globe communicate and create online in ways inextricably connected to cues, references, and in jokes that relate to the intricacies of their racial, ethnic and cultural identities".[31]

Social media operates in a global context. In this case, the process by which videos were collected via WhatsApp, stitched into a TikTok challenge, shared on Twitter and curated on YouTube, shows how in some ways tastes and activities may appear to transcend borders. However, it is also worth noting that although we are communicating with people in the global village, in a multitude of locations, that physical and virtual geographies still play a part. At the same time, power and politics in terms of the ownership and control of platforms retain a deep significance.[32] Also, online Black identities do reflect national, regional and local sensibilities, and this can be seen in the responses to the challenge. Furthermore, language, access and control remain issues, particularly as the ownership of platforms is not in the hands of afro-diasporic communities. Digital technology is not neutral or benign — it does not exist or operate outside of capitalist structures. As André Brock reminds us, it is important to remember that "Black folks lack material and financial control over the digital infrastructure".[33]

Writing from a South African perspective, feminist scholar Mbali Mazibuko explores the ways in which the #DontRushChallenge travelled from the UK via the United States to South Africa and argues that "the video caught the attention of many other Black women from across the globe and led to the unfolding of [...] a cultural moment". Mazibuko contends that, as Black women, the #DontRushChallenge was "a way to express ourselves in ways other than mourning".[34] For context, South Africa had a hard lockdown during the pandemic. President Ramaphosa declared a National State of Disaster on 15 March, followed by a national stay-at-home order issued on 23 March.[35]

Mbali Mazibuko makes the point that Black South African women used their own linguistic tools, including "*semhle*", a colloquial Xhosa word meaning "you are beautiful" that was mainly used on social media. *Semhle* acknowledged how Black women came together to create videos that showcased diverse forms of beauty.[36] Drawing on the work of digital media scholars Francesca Sobande and Krys Osei,[37] Mbali Mazibuko reminds us that the #DontRushChallenge may be interpreted as a community-based project, a method by which Black women can connect and express themselves. Within the context of a pandemic and lockdown, this form of visual communication becomes even more imperative. In pandemic time, the #DontRushChallenge provided a method for Black women to find ways to be in their community and experience joy. The question of what to do when "grief sits on our chest" during these times remains an important one, and articulating the value in celebrating and sharing online offers a meaningful response.[38]

Music Online as a Technology of the Self

Michel Foucault's concept of "technologies of the self" speaks to how we relate to and work with our bodies, thoughts and conduct to transform ourselves in order to attain a state of happiness.[39] Writing at a time before the widespread use of the internet, sociologist Tia DeNora reminds of us the of ways in which music works as a technology of the self — how we consume it allows us the space to reflect on who we are. Music forms an intrinsic part of care of the self — it blocks out other noise and provides a way to engage with the world.[40] In a multitude of towns and cities across the globe, people were singing, playing music and dancing while simultaneously contained inside, behind closed doors and deprived of collective activities.[41] For some, like the University of Hull students, the reaction to a subdued, indoor life was creative, sonorous and shared via digital spaces.

During the pandemic, music acted as a technology of the self as a way to manage mood and feelings of isolation. It was a way to alter, even if only for a short time, sentiments of sadness and confusion. The world as we knew it had changed suddenly, and as the social fabric had altered, many activities that joined us together were no longer an option.[42] By sharing music online, it was possible to reconnect with people outside of our immediate setting. At the same time, though, these sound initiatives gave new meaning to the spaces we found ourselves in, generating playful collective experiences that enabled us to build "sonic-musical territorialities"[43] where, online, we could make social connections and feel that society continued in some way. In pandemic time, fear was amplified by the media in this context of isolation. Constant broadcast of death tolls and infection rates by mainstream and social media contributed to an "imaginary of uncertainty and insecurity".[44] However, creating a "musical asylum" or bubble constituted an interesting survival strategy which allowed players to distance themselves a little from the avalanche of tragic or dystopian news that emerged on social networks and the media in general.[45] As we were temporarily removed from many of the social aspects of life, sound and music became even more important.

Throughout the lockdown periods, people watched their loved ones going to work, as key workers were on the front line in healthcare, social care, retail and delivery services. Post-lockdown but still in pandemic time, the physical and emotional effects continue to be exposed.[46] The repercussions of staying in and having little social contact, and the constant news bulletins about death and dying, are yet to be revealed fully, but no doubt they will be long-lasting. Somehow, we had to come to terms with widespread loss and grief, as well as the recognition that the death toll reflected existing racial and socio-economic inequalities.

Although the #DontRushChallenge connected communities around the globe in ways that were nourishing and fulfilling, it is worth remembering that in our digital age, online content is often created to generate views. Being watched or followed becomes a prime motivation in the way we live our lives online and offline. In ordinary times, the boundary between public and private is often blurred; in pandemic time, the need to be seen intensifies. Attention is a commodity, and often the content that is created is what essayist and cultural critic Jesse McCarthy refers to as a "voyeuristic event" that is then serially reproduced, shared and recreated (where possible) until the motif has been exhausted.[47] In a way that is typical for the rap genre, the lyrical content of "Don't Rush" alludes to and comments on sexual activities and drug use, as well as potentially criminal acts. Watching members of the US military[48] and police officers[49] transform themselves using their uniforms as props in combination with the song strikes a somewhat discordant note in this context.

However, the proliferation of social media, the internet and technology means that, as Zygmunt Bauman reminds us in *Liquid Times*, there is nothing left which is remote and unknowable.[50] As people and places are interconnected, it is unlikely that material (memes, images or indeed challenges) that have been shared online will stay within a particular realm. In a globalised world, cultural and creative practices are no longer confined to national borders. Contemporary Black musical forms are often viewed through a problematising lens.[51] By contrast, we can see how Black musical expression is always in motion, and constantly being reinvented. In this way, ludic opportunities for light-heartedness and joy emerge, and they were of particular relevance in pandemic time, when we were cut loose from everyday aspects of sociality.

In pandemic time, our activities were synchronised by the clock; nightly death announcements on the news featured as a gruesome spectacle. During that time, we sought ways to fill spaces that had suddenly become shapeless. The contours of everyday life shifted against a backdrop of death tolls and Covid-19 case counts. As the days, weeks and months passed, the world began to open up but with social restrictions in place. Separated from others and operating at a distance from our previous daily routines, we were for a time passengers in our own lives. We used music to pass the time, engaging in challenges and sharing sounds, as we tried to make memories of where we were and who we were.

The sociality of everyday life became something that

happened online. Our computer screens, Smart TVs and mobile phones provided a window to a world that we could not participate in in the same way. We became more used to seeing our faces, often for hours at a time. Previously noisy streets quietened down, city hustle and bustle was replaced by the sound of electric vehicles and delivery bikes. For a few weeks, the quietness was interrupted when we clapped for the NHS and for ourselves, applauding in time, on time, on Thursdays at eight.

Conclusion

In this chapter I have discussed how time changed shape during the early days of the pandemic, looking at ways that we passed the time online, with Black creative expression as a sonic backdrop to life online. An inherent relationship exists between Black cultural practice and socio-economic conditions. Rap in all its forms shows how Black aesthetics connect beyond national borders. Even if the corporations extract from it and dilute it, rap continues to belong to and speak to marginal, racialised communities. The emergence and subsequent rise of the internet and social media platforms broadened the reach of rap to a global audience. Rap resonates with people from vast and diverse backgrounds. It speaks to the everyday struggles of ordinary people's lives and points to a way out, on, or up. In pandemic time, it offered a backdrop for online activity when lives were being lived in isolation.

Rap formed the basis for dance crazes, memes and challenges. The #DontRushChallenge is an example of a sonic event for social media that subsequently went viral. An online activity to relieve boredom, created by a group of Black girls in Hull during the first month of lockdown, became a global sensation. Black women around the world participated as a way to connect with others during isolation and maintain social contact. Drawing on a South African perspective shows how despite the globalising nature of internet and social media, local and national identities are reflected in the challenge. As social life fragmented, engaging with music online was a way to manage the temporal changes to everyday life. Sharing music online was a way to stay connected, and both of these aspects work as a technologies of the self.

CHAPTER 3

MUSICKING IN PANDEMIC TIME

Life for musicians has always been precarious, and over the last fifteen or so years a technological advance has caused a shift in how musicians generate their income. Most do not earn money from recordings, but instead use a range of sources to make money. Although the music industry has long been an early adopter of technology — adapting its economic model with each technological advance — these innovations have not translated into increases in musicians' income.[1] In pandemic time, Covid-19 restrictions exacerbated musicians' precarity. Limits to creativity were stretched as the restrictions took hold, and accelerated and enhanced different ways to create, produce and share music. During this sudden and seemingly endless interruption, the relationship between artists and fans became more intense, more intimate and more demanding, as time weighed heavy for both the musician and their audiences.

The abrupt changes in those first days of the pandemic badly affected musicians and the music industry; both had to adapt quickly in light of closed venues and event cancellations. An immediate increase in online concerts and performances followed the imposition of the first wave of restrictions. As I have outlined in a previous chapter, the music economy lost large amounts of revenue and the government response to this loss of income was slow in comparison with other sectors of the creative and cultural industries. In the following days and weeks, as people became used to the restrictions, for some, staying at home became the new norm. For others, there was resistance and protest. More and more digital platforms emerged as musicians sought alternative ways to engage with their audiences. As well as individual artists finding other ways to perform,[2] corporate response included sponsored livestreamed events.[3]

Social Media

Although its main focus is on classical music, Christopher Small's concept of "musicking" brings together the many aspects of making, listening to and taking part in music.[4] Music operates as a universal form of communication, whilst at the same time being culturally specific and therefore evoking a sense of belonging and community. The connection between the musician and the audience is intimate, and in many ways social media makes it even more so. Fans can get up close to the artist and have a direct interaction with them. Boundaries are blurred not only between the artist and the audience, but also between time and space. In pandemic time, online interactions on platforms such as Zoom or Instagram helped to recreate and reimagine in-person music events, acting as a buffer to feelings of loneliness and isolation.[5]

Since the turn of the century, music lovers have been sharing and exchanging tunes online. Advances in technology — specifically digital and social media — have diversified the way we share and consume music. From the Myspace era of the mid-2000s to current social networking sites such as Facebook and Instagram, fans and artists can have a much more direct relationship. A culture of networked communities underpins our contemporary musical experience, and there is an expectation that we will be able to share our tastes and opinions. Social media platforms therefore have an important role to play in creating and maintaining these online musical relationships. Technological developments over the last few decades mean that the traditional way of people coming together in public in "communities of shared taste" is of less significance. Instead, what we experience is a more "mediated sociability", where being in a co-present community is not the only way to enjoy or take part in music. Fans can take part in an intimate but distanced relationship with an artist, engaging in a "non-reciprocal intimacy between a fan and a performer",[6] offering commentary and opinions, writing blogs, sharing photos and recordings. Online, digital interactions intensify these relationships across time and space as communities are formed across existing boundaries.

On social media, private listening and public performance are interwoven. Social media also gives the impression of ongoing activity. The complex algorithms of social media and streaming platforms have an impact on the ways in which fans engage with music.[7] Facebook, Twitter and Instagram, as well as music services like Spotify, feature profile pages and live feeds, as well as status updates. These online platforms share many features, including ongoing and invisible links between musicians and individual audience members, labelled connections and responses, multiple modes of interacting, some form of one-to-one communication, allowing to post updates (and then aggregating these into personalised feeds for each user), validated "official" accounts for musicians[8] and visible metrics of popularity, e.g., "friends", "followers", "fans".[9]

Artists can interact with their audience using sound, text, video and images. Fans can choose to take an active part or simply eavesdrop. Participating in some way allows for an online sociality, as well as a way to engage with others. Sharing music on social media requires us to imagine that there is an audience out there to listen,[10] so we upload in anticipation of finding kindred spirits and community. This became even more important in pandemic time, when the desire to maintain social ties became even more urgent.

Musicking in Online Contexts

In March 2020, when the world locked down, live performances went digital overnight, and by April we were attending online musical performances in our thousands. In May, by the time the prime minister announced a conditional plan to lift the lockdown in the UK, there had been months of remote and online concerts, shows and musical events — no standing in front of a stage, no in-person interaction with an audience.

Music provides us with a sense of space and time, and how we partake in a musical experience plays out in any combination of a number of ways, whether that is listening, moving, singing or dancing. However we choose to take part, our activities gesture towards a feeling of being in the world with others.[11] During the pandemic, with lockdown, isolation and social distancing, we had to find moments where we could be in community, often using music as a way to create and maintain social ties. In an online context, participation in cultural experiences as a musician and as an audience member shifted in shape and format.

Whether we log in to an international online event, listen to and engage with a soundtrack to a film, or participate in a live, in-person performance, we are actively taking part. I will now turn to three musical events that took place during the pandemic time that were presented in distinct formats: the Beenie Man v Bounty Killer *Verzuz* battle session (on social media via Instagram); *Lovers Rock*, part of the BBC *Small Axe* anthology series (on national television); and Dennis Bovell Presents a Night of Lovers Rock (an in-person event at the Southbank in London). I want to think through the ways in which the type of music and the purpose of it linked people together during pandemic time.

Beenie Man v Bounty Killer

Launched in 2020 by veteran music producers Swizz Beatz and Timbaland, one fairly early response to the lockdown restrictions' curtailing of live music events were the *Verzuz* "battle sessions" that took place online. The concept was two comparable music artists from Black music traditions (mainly hip hop and RnB) playing songs from their music catalogue in an alternating fashion.[12] Performers were not paid to take part. The contest was livestreamed on various platforms, including Instagram, Apple TV and Triller. The audience's role is to watch, comment and then offer an opinion on who had won the battle.

The first of these virtual competitions, between Timbaland and Swizz Beatz, took place via an Instagram Live broadcast in March 2020. Broadcasting thereafter every couple of days and featuring artist pairings such as Teddy Riley/Babyface and Erykah Badu/Jill Scott, early episodes took place under strict lockdown rules, with artists using their tablet or phone to take part. Although there were some issues with the technology at first, the audience grew steadily. In May 2020, when the Bounty Killer versus Beenie Man edition of *Verzuz* was broadcast, Boris Johnson was urging people to return to the office, but live music was still not happening, and nightclubs remained closed.

Beenie Man (Moses Anthony Davis) is a veteran of the dancehall scene from Kingston, Jamaica. Since the early 1990s, he has had a long career as a musician, with US hits such as "Romi", "Who Am I" and "Girls Dem Sugar". In 2000, he received a Grammy award for Best Reggae Album and in 2002 had a hit with Janet Jackson, "Feel It Boy". Bounty Killer (Rodney Basil Price) is also a longstanding dancehall DJ. As well as success in his own right over many years, he has recorded with artists such as Busta Rhymes, No Doubt, the Fugees, Mobb Deep and Swizz Beatz. A collaboration with No Doubt gave Bounty Killer a Grammy in 2002. Following a high-profile clash at Sting reggae festival in Jamaica in 1993, Beenie Man and Bounty Killer had a long-running rivalry until 2014, when they settled their dispute.

Taking place in Jamaica, where lockdown restrictions had been eased, Bounty Killer and Beenie Man did the battle in-person, but socially distanced and without a live audience.[13] Lasting approximately one hour and fifteen minutes, it was watched across the world, in the Caribbean, North America and Europe. In relation to the other *Verzuz* battles, this one was an outlier — the battles before this clash, and those that came after it, featured mainly North American RnB and hip-hop artists. Dancehall was a break in the sequence. Reggae as a genre comprises a number of musical styles, including roots and culture and dancehall.[14] However, while reggae is often seen as uplifting and socially conscious, articulating the struggles of the poor and marginalised, dancehall is characterised by digital beats and controversial lyrics.[15] Sonically, dancehall marks a separation from prior Jamaican musical forms such as mento, ska, dub and roots reggae.[16] Dancehall originally operated as a physical place to stage dances or events, as an alternative public sphere; it was a site for the sound clash — where respective sound systems could go back and forth lyrically and musically. Now it defines a genre of popular

Jamaican music that encompasses DJs, selectors, sound systems and dancers.

However, although dancehall is a popular musical form, it is not without its detractors. It has been demonised in Jamaica and in Britain as "perpetuating and promoting 'slackness'"[17] or vulgarity. The lyrics are often explicit and sexually suggestive, and dancehall events are often criminalised as sites of indecency and violence. Two decades ago, Carolyn Cooper argued that the numerous references to guns in the lyrical wordplay of dancehall tracks had criminalised not just the music, but the culture as well.[18] Nevertheless, dancehall extends beyond music into fashion, language, performance practice and politics.[19] Acting as an alternative public sphere, it is a site for the sound clash — where respective sound systems could debate lyrically and musically. As sociologist Lez Henry argues, chatting on the mic allows for a certain freedom, where an artist can freely critique anyone or anything.[20]

Beenie and Bounty performed against a traditional but adapted dancehall set-up. Two DJs and a videographer were also present. The DJ set was adorned with a Jamaican flag. Initially, both artists worked over rap beats and R&B sounds, then as the energy and tempo heightened they engaged in a lively back and forth, lyrical sparring. Both artists presented their biggest hits, commenting on collaborations with Pharrell (Beenie) and Wyclef Jean (Bounty) among others. At one point, the sponsor — a vodka company — is mentioned and a bottle is placed in view. Twenty three minutes into the clash, the music stops and Beenie Man announces, "The police are here!" He then conducts conversation with the officer who is out of shot and inaudible: "Good evening officer, we are live on international television, and the police are here [...] Do you want to be that guy?"

After a hiatus of a minute or so, the music starts again. It is a good-natured event, with much laughter and dancing throughout. Throughout the performance, the artists dance, the DJs and the videographer dance. The movement is as important as the lyrical expression, and both artists invoke the physicality of the dance, communicating through "symbolic gestures and kinesthetic action" to an audience they cannot see.[21] At thirty-five minutes, Bounty announces that Rihanna has tuned in, "Rih Rih is on the line, see we on her TV, Bounty Killa alongside Beenie." Towards the end of the session, the music backdrop changes again to soul, R&B and EDM.

Working in a very confined space, with only a few people in attendance, Beenie Man and Bounty Killer create a vibrant, energetic and enjoyable atmosphere. Half a million people watched the clash on Instagram, including a number of internationally well-known musicians like Rihanna, Skepta, Missy Elliot and Popcaan. Appreciative Instagram comments and emojis flow continuously throughout the set. An acknowledgment of Covid-19 and pandemic time comes at fifty-five minutes, when both artists offer condolences to those who have lost loved ones and implore the viewers to "tan ah yuh yaad" (stay at home).

This Verzuz clash brought us dancehall minus the physical space of the dance. As isolated individuals, we converged in a virtual set where the two DJs offered a temporary reprieve, an alternative space that made life a little more bearable, at least for a while. Throughout the diaspora, we were able to experience, from a distance, a resolutely Jamaican sonic happening that encompassed a communal practice of call-and-response and improvisation that is embodied in many Black musical cultures.[22]

Dancehall allows for the formulation of new identities that are able to critique a dominant Western narrative of propriety.[23] In this clash, there was very little "slackness" or lyrical violence in evidence; however, the "police interruption" during the set played into the ways in which dancehall has been positioned as an unruly subculture that needs to be carefully controlled. Despite these limits, and the constraints of being online, dancehall's resistant spirit still offers an emancipatory space.

Small Axe: Lovers Rock

Small Axe, by director Steve McQueen, presented "five insights into the lives of young Caribbean communities in London". The series aired over a five-week period during lockdown. Music featured heavily in *Lovers Rock*, the second film in the anthology. With a screenplay co-authored by McQueen and Courttia Newland, it is a story of young love set in 1980 with a blues party as its backdrop.[24] In the first three minutes, in anticipation of the main event, we see a group of women prepare food while singing an acapella version of Janet Kay's famous track "Silly Games".[25] Later on, "Silly Games" is called in again as an eleven-minute scene. The musician Dennis Bovell has a cameo role, and you can hear his vocals as the crowd sings. This scene, however, is one of many seen as inauthentic and contrived by those who actually experienced the blues dance parties of that time.

The title of the film is drawn from the musical genre, lovers rock, which sociologist Lisa Palmer tells us is the "tender romantic love songs that merged roots reggae basslines from Jamaica, the soulful melodies of Chicago and Philadelphia soul with a touch of British pop [...]. It was an early expression of a definitive Black UK sound".[26] Music producers Dennis Bovell and John Kpiaye — the originators of the lovers rock sound — wanted to find a distinct Black British reggae that went beyond imitating the sounds which were coming out of Jamaica. Palmer locates the emergence of the genre in Thatcher's Britain and explains the ways in which the socio-cultural impact of lovers rock and "conscious roots reconfigure the stereotypical, loveless, and nihilistic representations of their identities found in popular discourse".[27] As well as being a method for loving Blackness, it created a space for Black feminine joy. Drawing on the work of Paul Gilroy, Palmer reminds us that lovers rock was also a transnational project: "Lovers Rock is [...] a distinctly transnational cultural project emerging from the creative, political and erotic impulses of Caribbean communities in Britain."[28] Although its popularity peaked by the early 1980s, as a genre it has a nostalgic and contemporary engagement, with a steady supply of live events running throughout the year.

The first film in the *Small Axe* series, *Mangrove*, had been broadcast the week before and was well received. It told a key narrative of Black resistance in Britain. As the next film in the sequence, *Lovers Rock* was keenly anticipated, generating commentary on social media prior to and during broadcast. As a visual and sonic event, it attracted an intergenerational audience. For younger viewers, it provided an opportunity for conversations about historical Black life. However, for those who were of that time, who had experienced the era and therefore had a profound investment in lovers rock as a genre, key aspects missed the mark. It provoked some strong feelings and some backlash. Looking through the online responses and commentary illustrates a shared experience, but reactions are mixed, as the comments on social media showed:

#SmallAxe #LoversRock has had me feeling emotional in a way I can't describe today. Our culture really is sacred. The extraction & harm of our people is attempting to break something sacred. But look how beautiful we are. How beautiful our culture is.

The direction. The cinematography. The music. The looks. The style. The fashions.

And in reply to the two tweets above:

Just perfect. Loved it. Getting texts from my mum reminiscing the days that she went to blues parties growing up. We are miles away, but both tuned in. Seeing authentic history on TV, as your parents lived it .

However, not all viewers agreed:

Well #smallaxe #LoversRock this was complete rubbish and I can't believe what I just saw. No storyline of note and totally misrepresented the time and the genre. I never see people ah gwaan like wild beast in ah party from the day mi born and even the music never save it VEX.

And in response:

Completely agree. Very disappointing. Research needs to be more thorough. I don't recognize some of what went on, seemed more like a Kumina situation. Nice nostalgia though.

And on Facebook:

For the record what I witnessed last night "Lovers Rock" was absolutely NOT a reflection of our parties!! It was a disgrace. I am so disappointed 😔 Anyone who feels the same should complain to BBC and use social media to let Steve know. That was NOT anywhere near the standard I've come to expect from him. I'm so upset about this rubbish. What a missed opportunity 🙁

Dennis Bovell Presents a Night of Lovers Rock

As summer arrived, lockdown was lifted, and we were allowed back outside. On 16 July 2021, I went to Dennis Bovell Presents a Night of Lovers Rock at the Southbank, outside on the riverside terrace. Dennis Bovell, the co-founder of the lovers rock genre who had a cameo in *Lovers Rock*, was the DJ, and the event featured live performances of songs from Janet Kay, Carroll Thomson and Victor Romero Evans.[29] It continued a long tradition of live lovers rock events that had been taking place in a number of formats for many years. We had to book in advance, numbers were strictly controlled, and we had to complete the Test and Trace documentation.[30] As we were still under social restrictions, no singing or dancing was allowed, and we had to remain seated at all times. Here is the guidance from the website:

> Due to the extended coronavirus restrictions there is reduced capacity for today's events. Entry is on a first come, first served basis, with a maximum seated capacity of 200. Audiences must be seated to watch the performances. Our site tends to be busier in good weather, and less so if it rains.[31]

Early on in the evening, while Dennis Bovell DJed, he sang a reggae version of Louis Armstrong's "What a Wonderful World". Later on, Carroll Thompson sang a number of tracks, including two of her greatest hits: "Simply in Love" and "Hopelessly in Love". By the time Janet Kay graced us with "Silly Games", it took great willpower to stay seated and obey the rules. We were not supposed to sing, but the audience sang their hearts out. We were not allowed to dance (but some of us did anyway). Three days later, on 19 July, most legal limits on social contact were removed.

Black Joy

In their conference paper "Finding Space for Black Joy in Live Music During COVID-19",[32] the authors identified a "double pandemic" for Black communities, where racial inequalities and racial discrimination increased the odds of contracting and dying from Covid-19. Although they are discussing the US, similar points could be made with regard to the UK, where some ethnic groups were disproportionately affected by the pandemic.[33] The subsequent loss and grief had a significant impact on wellbeing during pandemic times; however, "Black joy" provides a site of resistance and allows us to think beyond the contours of everyday life. Within the context of a global health crisis, Black joy takes on a particular significance.

How people make sense of the world in general, and specifically in pandemic time, often involves a constant interpretation and reinterpretation of space, entity and context. Black joy emerges from different spaces at a macro, meso and micro level. In other words, African-American, US and global cultures; music and social media; and lastly, in the micro spaces of performance such as the *Verzuz* battles and the small live events that took place as restrictions eased.[34] During the pandemic, Black joy was built on musical forms that provided "the basis for community, ritual, and myth".[35] Within this context, it is possible to see how the *Verzuz* battles operated as a trusted space of Black joy. What the battles offered was a portal to an online musical community at a time when people had experienced many weeks of lockdown and isolation.

As a genre, dancehall creates a communal space that is simultaneously hyper-individual, collective and collaborative.

As an example of Black Atlantic creative expression, dancehall flows through the diaspora and thus provides a collective experience for Afro-diasporic communities, as seen in the Beenie Man and Bounty Killer *Verzuz* battle, which had an intergenerational audience and included fans and musicians from across the diaspora.[36] In this online space, technology and art come together, offering a powerful mode of shared communication at a time when staying in and being confined had become the new normal.

Musicking in Uncertain Times

Music has the potential to enrich people's lives, and in pandemic time it was a key factor in how we kept ourselves occupied. Although restrictions eased at various points, there was a pressing need to pass the time in ways that kept us emotionally whole. During a unique situation, with a deadly virus in the air and being confined to our homes, music takes on even more significance as it forms a basis for individual relationships as well as collective, public experiences. In contemporary times, the advent and proliferation of social media means that often private self and public self are intertwined. In *Why Music Matters*, David Hesmondhalgh notes how musical experiences — for example, listening to a song or watching a live performance — can be intensified if we know that others are sharing that experience too.[37] Music contributes to self-identity, as well as a sense of belonging and collective identity.

Although it can unite people across space and time, music is also susceptible to systemic change, such as "increasing consumerism, commodification and competitiveness".[38] Musicians in contemporary Black music genres have always operated from a place of scarcity, hence the initial DIY nature of many contemporary Black musical forms.[39] Over time, it has become more and more apparent that only the most privileged young people are able carve out careers as professional musicians.

In our neoliberal era, Afro-diasporic musical genres have been affected by commercialisation and globalisation. While music can bring people together and contribute to a sense of human flourishing, it may also be a way to obscure or play down unequal socio-economic conditions. As Nancy Baym points out, music "may serve as a sedative that numbs us to conditions we should be fighting, or maybe become a vehicle for individualistic competition".[40]

Musicking: Online, on Television, in Person

As an activity, "musicking" may include listening, watching, making, ad-libbing, commenting on, discussing and sharing music. Often the distinction between performance and participation is blurred — even more so when the performance takes place online. In an ethnographic study of the music-sharing practices of Spanish migrants in London, ethnomusicologist Raquel Campos Valverde extends musicking to include the concept of "imagined listening", "a form of sociality based on how we think others listen to music".[41] Valverde uses it as a tool to explain the social relationships that arise from people's interaction with online music, sharing as a way to articulate their cultural identity as well as make connections.

In online musicking, there is a shift from recorded music that you had to physically search for to music (of all kinds) at your fingertips that is constantly available. Sometimes the algorithm chooses for you. No crate-digging is required to discover new genres, sounds or tunes. We have moved away from discussion in print or in person about musicians and their music, and our comments go out into the world at a greater volume and at a rapid tempo. Algorithms create and shape audiences without human intervention, which gives the illusion of nonstop human activity.[42] Indeed, the music that people share and circulate may well be in response to their algorithmic prompts.[43] At the same time, discussions and commentary about music, such as the one that took place after the *Lovers Rock* screening, have a particular intensity. In the case of *Lovers Rock*, some viewers anticipated and expected an authenticity that the title of the film promised but could not provide. In many ways, the context of being locked in, coupled with intergenerational communities "watching together", contributed to the discord amongst the imagined audience.

During pandemic time, the urge to stay in contact with family and friends intensified as many of our connections moved online. Our interactions often took the form of sharing (or co-engaging in) musical choices, tastes and events. An upsurge in the number and variety of digital platforms provided new ways to produce and disseminate creative content of all kinds. Although being online allowed amateur and professional musicians to maintain an artistic presence and recoup some of their lost income from the closure of clubs and festivals, at the same time, online efforts, particularly in the early days of lockdown, lacked atmosphere. Live performance relies on a two-way flow between the artist and the audience to generate a vibe, regardless of the online platform. In lockdown, musicians were giving concerts to an audience that they could not see.

For DJs and MCs, the online space took on a different shape. Writing about livestreaming of sets during pandemic time, Adam de Paor-Evans notes that online there was a less clear distinction between the private space of the DJ booth and the public spaces of the dancefloor or the bar that you would get at an in-person event.[44] DJs were often broadcasting from their homes, offering a view into a previously unseen element of the DJ's world. Audience participation by way of fire emojis and typed notes in the comments could not adequately replace the physical response to the sounds, gestures and movements that would happen in person.

Clubs and festivals had little choice but to move to an online format, which enabled them to generate some — albeit very reduced — income. The emergence of multiple digital platforms meant fierce competition for attention, and many events were provided at low or no cost. Free performances and unpaid work in the music industry has deep implications, as it reduces paid opportunities and ultimately further devalues what people are likely to pay to consume music.[45]

Once we were back outside, no singing or dancing at live events changed the nature of what a music event looked and felt like. An expectation to be seated and remain so was the new norm, while the crush at the bar became a distant memory, replaced by table service via a QR code.

Conclusion

Music connects people across space and time. Aside from listening and playing, all aspects of musicking provide us with joy. In periods of uncertainty and discomfort, music can enhance individual and collective wellbeing.[46] In this chapter, I have reflected on three musical interludes that I engaged with during the pandemic where that connection occurred: the *Verzuz* clash between Beenie Man and Bounty Killer; the BBC television film *Lovers Rock*; and finally, when we were provisionally allowed back outside, a free, in-person concert at the Southbank in London, Dennis Bovell Presents a Night of Lovers Rock.

The sonic events that I have foregrounded here in this chapter illustrate how, during long periods of confinement, we needed social media and digital technology more than ever. What it also shows is how being in *communitas* —

sharing an atmosphere and a sense of intimacy — is a definitive experience that cannot be easily reproduced online. Live events provide a source of sociality that adds to our wellbeing. While online discussions may boost our enjoyment of a musical event, being placed in conversation with others who have vastly differing perspectives may add to feelings of dislocation, disconnection and discomfort.

Aside from this aspect, digital technological advances do not always live up to their emancipatory promise, and we cannot divorce their impact from wider society. The popularity and necessity of social media and the internet takes place within the contours of socio-economic inequality; it highlights existing patterns of injustice relating to class, race, gender, age and geographical location. A precarity of experience and earnings, in other words working for longer hours and less money to provide media content and build a brand, has adversely affected musicians' mental health and wellbeing.[47] As a site where livelihoods have been irrevocably affected, the music industry holds up a mirror to other economic sectors where technology was supposed to free us.[48] Creative work — including music — is now an uncertain, precarious task, and Covid-19 has further highlighted and exacerbated this.

However, as the global pandemic set off new patterns of disadvantage, it also heightened awareness of social, economic and racial injustice. Two days after the Beenie Man/Bounty Killer *Verzuz* clash, George Floyd was murdered by the Minneapolis police — a horrible, tragic event that generated months of protest, online and in person. Corporations — including the music industry — were urged to respond to racial inequality, leading to a raft of rapid responses, many of which were short-lived.[49] Racial injustice and terror was marketised, commodified and broadcast to communities who were locked in and socially isolated.

Although some would argue that the ability of Afro-diasporic music to promote interaction and solidarity to enhance collective flourishing has been lost,[50] I have shown in this chapter the critical importance of participating in music in all its forms. Being able to share musical experiences online meant that we still had a connection to each other in some way, offering a "musical sociability" that takes on a deep significance in times of isolation. Even when restrictions were eased, we were still limited in how we could connect with one another. Small in-person events allowed a repurposed form of musical sociability — strengthening our sense of what we had in common with each other.

CHAPTER 4
SONIC BLACK GEOGRAPHIES

Normally, I am a "big speakers" listener — I like the sound to surround me, to be in the air. But during pandemic time, I adapted my listening habits. Before lockdown, I used headphones only for news or audiobooks, and usually when I wanted to block out external noise. In the early days of the pandemic, making use of the one hour of permitted exercise meant long walks, and I learned to appreciate consuming music in that format. Walking through unusually quiet, East London streets while listening to new music from Ghetts, I was struck by how I experienced a sense of place on two levels, the real — underneath my feet — and the imaginary, which came into view with the help of the lyrics.

In her book *Demonic Grounds*, Katherine McKittrick reminds us that the relationship between Black populations and geography is an important one. Thinking about space, place and location — both physical and imagined — allows us to engage with narratives that foreground social lives which are often rendered invisible.[1] Black geographies, as Professor Pat Noxolo points out, operate in two directions at the same time, from personal reflections on local circumstances to critiques of national and/or global conditions.[2] For a long time, Black diaspora populations have been "telling how their surroundings have shaped their lives",[3] and Black geographies centre these accounts.

Rap as a globally popular Black musical form provides a sonic backdrop to the pandemic time that is the focus of this chapter. As a by-product of post-industrial urban environments, rap speaks to the everyday struggles of ordinary people's lives. Sonic Black geographies in this context relate to the ways in which two distinct iterations of rap — grime and UK drill — dispensed social commentary that spoke to local and global conditions at a time of lockdown and social restriction.

Introducing Grime and UK Drill

Emerging at the turn of the twenty-first century, grime is a contemporary Black British musical genre with its roots in East London. As such, it provides an anchor and an entry point to a contemporary Black British history that is often muted or invisible. Grime sounds like where it is from — the street corners and council estates of inner-city East London. It draws from an eclectic mix of sounds structured around 140 beats per minute. Its sonic origins flow through the musical practices of the Black diaspora, namely hip-hop, reggae (particularly dancehall), jungle and UK garage. We can hear how reggae and dancehall have influenced grime in a number of ways, but I would highlight the sound clash, the role of the crew and "spitting" or rapping over a beat.[4]

In Jamaica, sound systems played a variety of music, with reggae at the core. UK-based sound systems also played many styles of music, including RnB, soul and UK garage. It is this sonic influence that can be heard in early grime, when it was evolving into its own genre out of UK garage.[5] What is also clear is that the family and kinship connections from reggae to grime are of critical importance. Back in the mid-2000s, when I interviewed people from the grime scene, performers often talked about the influence of reggae on their own work. Reggae and dancehall framed the sonic landscape of their formative years, disseminated via relatives who were also involved in music in some way. Many performers had relatives that were DJs, ran sound systems, were singers, musicians and so on. In the early grime days, crews were often fluid entities — what bound them together was a love for music. There were also often family connections and kinship ties, with members who attended the same schools, grew up on the same estates or were brothers or relatives of some kind.

As a diaspora cultural form, influenced by hip-hop, jungle, dancehall and UK garage, grime has been nourished by its ongoing Black Atlantic connections to the Caribbean, Africa and North America.[6] Although it came of age in the YouTube era, from 2005 onwards, grime's original stomping ground was pirate radio, which offered a unique opportunity for young DJs and MCs to put in their practice hours.[7] Pirate radio stations played the music that young people wanted to hear, in a way that they wanted to hear it, with requests and shout-outs, as well as information regarding upcoming events. Pirate radio was a way to hear the latest tunes, listen to favourite DJs and find out what was going on.[8] Pirate radio had a certain vibe, and brought a different energy to what was available. When the BBC wanted to take some of the staleness out of their output, they set up 1Xtra to emulate what the pirates were doing, often taking on former pirate radio DJs. For the police and the regulating authorities, pirates were simply a criminal nuisance, as were grime events, which were often shut down.

Along the way, and despite some bumps in the road, grime became big business. By using English accents, and therefore their own voice, grime provided young Black Britons an opportunity to step away from the "elders" in the UK garage scene, who at the time were not paying too much attention. From this came the liberating aspect that can occur in a liminal space where young people can have fun as well as talk about their everyday lives, struggles and aspirations. All of this developed out of a sound system culture that was the sonic background for many MCs. As an ecosystem of live performance and events, as well as the production and sale of music and merchandise, grime shares a continuity of practice with sound system culture.

During its foundational years, in a time of scarce resources, rap adopted a DIY approach to music-making, using machines — turntables, tape machines and sound systems — in ways for which they were not intended. Rap's focus is on the rhythm and the sound, using repetition and musical breaks in innovative ways.[9] The early adoption and inventive use of digital samplers allowed for the development of rap as a "technologically sophisticated and complex urban sound".[10] In a similar way, participants in the grime scene drew on a cultural heritage and creative practice that came via VHS video tapes[11] and recorded audio cassettes of Jamaican sound systems.[12]

In its early years, grime utilised its own distinct marketing routes — relying on flyers, pirate radio and word of mouth to publicise events. However, in the early internet era, the dissemination of grime was supplemented by Myspace and Facebook, digital TV and YouTube,[13] as well as online platforms dedicated to grime, including SBTV (2006), Linkup TV (2008) and GRM Daily.[14] The journey from Channel U to MTV Base, bringing grime to a wider audience, was also an important development.[15]

Police crackdowns on live grime events in London meant that performance locations for this creative expression spread outwards, and technological advances allowed for audiences to be established first in the London suburbs, then across the UK and beyond.[16] As more social media platforms emerged, artists used Twitter, Instagram and Snapchat, for example, as everyday promotional tools.

The subsequent emergence and spread of drill and UK drill reflects the changes in technology as well as the music industry. Music is constantly available on a multitude of platforms, with fans able to comment and share at a rapid pace. Drill artists recognised the possibilities of this early on, having seen the material success of Chief Keef, whose breakthrough track took him up and out of poverty.[17] In this new landscape, what Forrest Stuart calls "a drillers world", the artist is competing for attention on the internet and has a tacit understanding of how the algorithms work.[18] Both grime and UK drill have been positioned as unruly subcultures underpinned by an aesthetic that is steeped in violence. Both also have a visual formation that may include large groups of young men, incorporating specific gestures and poses that are often read as aggressive.[19] For drillers, the taunts and challenges form an intrinsic part of the lyrical method.[20] As a result, UK drill is often associated with crime, violence and disorder.

Regulating authorities, including the police and local councils, came down forcefully on a genre that is made predominantly by young Black people.[21] An easy association with "gangs" and "gang-related activity" often goes hand in hand with the making and sharing of drill, and in a social media era, surveillance techniques and tools are brought to bear.[22] The online creation and sharing of music therefore becomes less liberatory in this aspect, and more about monitoring and control.[23] Grime created a unique sound, laying a sonic, DIY foundation for UK drill to follow.[24] While grime emerged in an analogue time via pirate radio, record shops and raves, and then came of age in the internet age with YouTube and social media, UK drill is a mainly an online phenomenon.

Drill — originally a musical genre from the South Side of Chicago — has been in existence since the late 1990s.[25] However, it was Chief Keef's viral video for "I Don't Like" that brought it to a wider audience.[26] In the UK, a version by JME, Jammer and Skepta, following in the sonic pattern laid out by grime, swiftly followed.[27]

In *Street Illiteracy Decoded*, criminologist Jonathan Ilan outlines how UK drill as a specific iteration of Chicago drill established a foothold in London from around 2012.[28] Since then, UK drill has gained popularity throughout the UK. UK drill artists have used the templates established by the grime music economy, also utilising social media platforms to disseminate their creative output and build fan bases that extend far beyond their immediate location. Artists use YouTube, for example, to create channels to share their songs, offering fans an opportunity to comment on and discuss the work.

The drill aesthetic utilises covered faces — artists often wear balaclavas, masks or other face coverings. Locations are from an inner-city perspective: side roads, car parks, often at night — even if shot outdoors there is a claustrophobic feel. Forrest Stuart, in his *Ballad of the Bullet: Gangs, Drill Music, and the Power of Online Infamy*, offers a reading of drill as "an emerging genre of hyperviolent, hyperlocal, DIY-style gangsta rap that claims to document street life and violent criminality".[29] In a UK context, criminologists Craig Pinkney and Shona Robinson-Edwards argue that the "drill phenomenon is clearly intertwined with violence".[30] However, as the genre has evolved, the content has in some ways become more nuanced, as artists insert humour as well as social commentary into their songs.[31]

As an online musical form, drill rappers have a tacit knowledge of social media algorithms and how to use them effectively to promote their work.[32] Stuart, however, foregrounds the nihilistic and often damaging aspects of creating drill:

Through music videos and other social media uploads these 'drill rappers' [...] compete on a global stage to prove that they're more ruthless, more delinquent, and more authentic than their competitors.[33]

Other readings of drill emphasise the social commentary with respect to material conditions,[34] a deeper understanding of violence and capitalism,[35] resistance,[36] the construction of identity[37] and opportunities to develop creative skills and careers.[38]

Post-Industrial Decline: Contextualising the "Ends"

Multicultural communities are a longstanding feature of inner-city life in the UK.[39] At the same time, these areas experience poverty, inequality and economic hardship. Since the 1980s, the pursuit of neoliberal economics on both sides of the Atlantic via Thatcherism and Reaganomics, as well as increasing globalisation, has led to diminishing economic opportunities for marginalised communities. As industry declined, inner cities were abandoned and often became sites of advanced marginality.[40] The subsequent "war on crime" actually became a war on poor neighbourhoods as marginalised communities became subject to increased control. Exacerbated by more than a decade of an "austerity agenda" that decimated public services, inequality has widened the gap between rich and poor. Consequently, in the inner cities, great wealth and extreme poverty often exist side by side.

In *Black Noise: Rap Music and Black Culture in Contemporary America* Tricia Rose defines rap as a culturally expressive response to the racialised deindustrialisation of urban America — a definition that could be used to describe to Black music in the UK.[41] The contemporary Black music forms that I focus on in this chapter — rap, grime and UK drill — have been formed in a crucible of post-industrial decline, hostility and inequality. In the diaspora, the Black communities from which these musical forms emerge constitute a geographic story, one that contains "placements and displacements, segregations and integrations, margins and centers, and migrations and settlements".[42] In other words, it is important to place the emergence of these musical forms into the context of migration from the Caribbean and Africa into the inner city at a time of post-industrial decline, taking into account the Black Atlantic flow of musical expression.

The colloquial term the "ends" is used by young people in urban settings to denote local, familiar neighbourhoods. A focus on what is lacking in the "ends", in terms of material goods and a perceived lack of socio-economic aspiration, misses the sense of belonging, comfort and street capital that these localities offer. The "ends" are places that provide validation, recognition, stability and safety, as well as the more commonly posited repressive geographies.[43] Locality matters — it contributes to a sense of self and informs the way that people present themselves to others. In this context, locality is an actively created, mediated space where young people, supported by technology, use the cultural construction of the "ends" to create personas that have purpose, power and meaning. In disadvantaged communities, life is often organised around the practical aspects of getting by. Within this habitus, there is a pervasive theme of making money and being able to provide for oneself and others. Young people's desire to be seen to be as a success leads to the pursuit of recognition, reputation and monetary reward, and this also plays out within the rap music sector.

In these marginalised communities, being "on road" or "road life" is constituted through the act of hanging out on a street corner or housing estate, and maybe participating in some level of illicit activity. While some scholars suggest that being "on road" is a liminal space where there is sovereignty and agency as well as freedom from a hostile society,[44] it has also been argued that it can be a collection of "panicky, chaotic, adrenalin-filled experiences" where young people exist in a hyper-aware state.[45] Communities move through inner city spaces in different ways; some enjoy a relatively unfettered and hazard-free experience, not usually curtailed by representatives of the state. Rod Earle described this group as a "kinetic elite". On the other hand, the young and/or racially marginalised in these areas belong to a "kinetic underclass", where they are under surveillance by the state and regulating authorities.[46]

Post-industrial urban decline also features in sociologist Yusef Bakkali's concept of *"munpain"* (mundane pain) — a term he uses to describe the everyday social suffering of contemporary life in the "ends".[47] Road life does not necessarily involve crime, but it is often framed in this way.[48] Recent iterations of rap such as grime and UK drill have been seen as contributing to the pull of road life and its inherent criminal acts.[49] In his important work, Bakkali reminds us to discard tired social media memes and videos that offer "stereotypical depictions of the 'road man' as stupid, savage and inherently violent", which ignore or render invisible the everyday existential and social death that many experience.[50] Looking at "road life" via a different lens, criminologist Ebony Reid uses narrative biographical accounts of men "on road" to outline "trap life" as a unique conceptual tool. Criminal motivations are placed within the context of material struggle and emotional pain. This is a useful concept that allows us to consider the psychological "trap" of feeling confined and yet unable to escape specific circumstances which in many ways may be damaging and dangerous.[51]

For young people from "ends", music may be a possible way out of "road life" and "trap life". At the same time, popularity and visibility through music might mean coming under the view of the regulating authorities, which for some rappers may lead to a more precarious position. Nevertheless, once this movement has been made, there is the potential for transformation to occur, not only of the environment that has been left, temporarily or permanently, but also of the individual, who is in some way altered by this process. It is evident that for young Black people from poor communities, participation in the contemporary music economy enables a shift away from the contours of the "ends".[52] However, "success" does not shield from everyday surveillance and control: at the height of his success, police forced entry into grime MC Stormzy's house[53]; Brixton drill duo Skengdo and AM were given a suspended prison sentence for playing one of their own songs which "allegedly incited violence against rival gang members"[54]; and in 2020, UK drill rapper Digga D was threatened with recall[55] for attending a Black Lives Matter protest.[56]

Grime, Rap and UK Drill as Social Commentary

The convivial activities of working-class inner-city youth are underpinned in part through a productive tension between local and global influences. Participants in this economy draw on complex diasporic connections of their lived experience in the UK, while at the same time commenting on life and creating music that goes beyond national borders.

After forty years of neoliberalism, hyper-individualism has become the common-sense narrative, and it is no wonder, then, that the mystical allure of meritocratic achievement and success runs through the music and the lyrics of grime and UK drill artists. As commercialisation is woven into the fabric of these genres, the temptation is to stop there; however, these iterations of rap continue in some way to articulate the struggles of the poorest and least represented.[57] Even if transformation through musical success is made possible, artists (and the communities that they are part of) continue to come up against systemic and structural racism. Success does not mitigate the performance and practice of racism[58]; it does not necessarily mean escape, and rappers continue to occupy a position straddled between "social vulnerability and clout"[59] where success is possible — but the risk remains of coming up against the criminal justice system. Beyond the posturing and boasting, a sense of identity, belonging and exposition of lived material conditions is at the heart of much of this work. In these intense conversations, it is possible to hear attempts to make sense of institutions and systems, the impact on personal wellbeing, everyday behaviour and how that relates to life in the "ends". Performing grime, rap and UK drill allows individuals to display a sonic rendering of their environment.[60]

In the UK, the boundaries and borders between grime and UK drill have become more blurred over time. Artists will work over different types of beat, moving back and forth between different genres. What I'm saying here is that this offers a unique perspective and social commentary on life in the UK, both with the experiences of the artists in real life and in the music that they put out. One example of commentary where art and life collide is "BLM" by UK drill collective OFB, which was released in the aftermath of the police killing of George Floyd. Rapping over a sample from Coldplay's "Trouble", Bandokay, Double Lz and Abra Cadabra highlight incarceration, police brutality and coming up against an unjust criminal justice system. For Bandokay, it is especially poignant, as in 2011 his father, Mark Duggan, was shot and killed by police, an act which sparked days of civil unrest.[61]

In February 2021, Ghetts — a musician who works across a number of genres, including grime — released his third studio album, *Conflict of Interest*.[62] The track "IC3" features north London MC Skepta and speaks to the challenges and contradictions of being a young Black man in Britain.[63] A collective amnesia that ignores Britain's colonial past and that cannot reconcile belonging with Black skin means that the particular refrain of "go back to where you came from" is levelled at Black people, wherever they were born. Ghetts refuses this, instead foregrounding Britain's role as a colonising project: "Don't tell me go back where I came from, while the Queen sits there in stolen jewels". Although Ghetts has achieved sufficient material success to move out of the "ends", he recognises that for many the struggle continues, and for him, he can never fully escape. In his verse, Skepta, formerly of grime crew Boy Better Know (BBK), talks about refusing an MBE, preferring instead to take up a chieftaincy in Nigeria.

"Teardrops", taken from Kano's album *Hoodies All Summer*, was first released in 2019, but its music video was first aired at GRM Daily Rated Awards in June 2020, which due to lockdown restrictions took place online.[64] Kano, like Ghetts, is from East London, and is a longstanding MC who defies categorisation. The music video is a short story of police brutality — the main character is stopped by the police because he is "in a nice car" and the area is "frequented by gangs". A hard-hitting visual, it graphically shows a violent response from the police, and in the last minute lists the number of Black people who had died in police custody as of that date.

Dave is another artist who moves within and between musical genres, including rap and UK drill. In July 2021, Dave released his second studio album, *We're All Alone in This Together*, focusing on themes of mental health, loneliness and the challenges for young Black lives in the inner city. On one track, "Three Rivers", Dave opts for a more traditional rap beat to reflect on the last sixty years of Britain's migration stories. Incorporating aspects of the Windrush story,[65] it features voices of people who were caught up in the midst of the scandal. On the same track, Oscar-winning actor Daniel Kaluuya talks about "switching rivers" as a metaphor for a psychic shift from experiencing "Black" as an obstacle, to seeing "Black" as an asset.[66]

Headie One started out as a member of drill group OFB, and is one of its early prominent artists, often collaborating with fellow north London rapper RV. In the early 2010s, Headie One released several mixtapes as an independent, eventually signing to Relentless Records. "Cold" is a track from Headie One's debut album *Edna*, named after his mother, who died when he was three.[67] Featuring Kaash Paige, an RnB singer from Dallas, Texas who came to attention via TikTok,[68] Headie One talks about coming up from the struggle, from council flat life, minimal resources, low expectations from teachers, but now he's doing so well he's "dodging his accountant". He alludes to his challenges with the criminal justice system, "Hung jury, no retrial", as well as indicating that material gains do not mitigate against hurt, "Quarter mil' in jewellery still don't stop a ni**a feelin' pain". In addition, when you are from "ends", any move you are able to make is progress: "I'm tellin' them, 'The sky and above,' when they ask me, 'What's next?' Cah every step is progress when you come from the trench."

TeeZandos is a drill rapper from Hackney in East London. In 2019, as a seventeen-year-old, her track "Need Focus" was an underground hit.[69] Using a classic drill aesthetic, TeeZandos tells a stylised story of "trapping" that, although it may or may not contain some kernels of truth, it is almost cartoonish in its portrayal. In an interview with *Vice* magazine, she discusses being signed to a label at the age of fourteen, as well as the experience of living a peripatetic lifestyle and the impact of having a father that went to jail.[70] She gestures towards using her music to shine a light on aspects of life in the "ends":

> The more I listen to drill, the more I think, it's not just boys [who] are doing this. I got to show people what's going on. I wasn't even allowed to rap drill when I signed to GB [Records] because I was young.

In December 2021, towards the end of the pandemic period, TeeZandos released "OT", a short, direct narrative that purports to tell her earlier life story.[71] Although the content is harsh in nature, it is catchy, easy on the ear and includes dance moves that may be readily reproduced on social media platforms such as TikTok.

Conclusion

Drawing on a sonic geography that incorporates musical flows to and from the Caribbean, the United States and Africa, grime emerged in East London in the early 2000s. UK drill, on the other hand, with a more direct route from South Side Chicago, was taken up by young Black people in the inner city and reworked for the UK, underpinned by a grime production aesthetic. According to economist Jacques Attali, "Art bears the mark of its time."[72] For grime MCs and UK drill rappers, their time is couched in social, economic and racial inequality, repressive state systems, a hostile environment and Britain's refusal to confront or address its imperialist and colonial past. All of which leaves Black Britons with an existential challenge in terms of creating a sense of belonging and identity. Black as an identity is no longer a singular unifying framework.[73] Black, in the context of these music scenes, means to connect to a Caribbean or African heritage while being located in and informed by being in the UK, creating a productive tension between local and global influences. In addition, as Katherine McKittrick points out, for Afro-diasporic communities the idea of belonging to a place or nation is incomplete while there is still a struggle for "socio-spatial liberation", living in a hostile environment where they are often adversely affected by institutional and systemic racism.[74]

The artists that I have foregrounded here illustrate how Black Britons' lived experience is informed by the doubleness of being in Britain, while at the same time looking in the direction of Africa and the Caribbean. Ghetts, Kano, Skepta, Headie One, TeeZandos and Dave draw on and collaborate with a multitude of Afro-diasporic heritages, including Jamaica, Nigeria and Ghana. Within this Black Atlantic context, cultural expression does not flow in line within national borders — instead it moves back and forth, crossing boundaries in myriad sonic iterations.[75] Geographer Rita Gayle reminds us that the "song" or the "tune" fills Black spaces and inspires moments which speak to Black women's exclusion and erasure. Although she is writing about lovers rock, I would extend this to UK drill too, as in some ways it provides a method for artists such as TeeZandos to speak to Black women's experiences. Also, sociologist Corey Miles makes an important point regarding how trap music offers a structure to understand felt experience "historically, biographically and materially".[76] Regardless of genre, Black music embodies resistance, operating as a site where, as Gayle suggests, "Blackness as song, like Blackness as people moves across fabricated boundaries [...] a movement that is in conflict with Britain's efforts to restrain Black culture".[77]

Since its inception, rap has become a significant cultural and economic force.[78] It speaks to and for the social, economic and political concerns of marginalised communities. In the UK, it is evident that rap has, to some extent, decentred pop as commercial viability is established, and the "mainstream" has taken notice.[79] In 2020, according to the British Phonographic Industry, UK rap (including grime and UK drill) accounted for almost a quarter of all singles purchases in Britain.[80] Over the last five decades, the innovative use of technology has hastened the dissemination and reworking of rap in different forms. So while it speaks to and for the social, economic and political concerns of marginalised communities, it also resonates with a much wider audience. What this means is that for young people from "ends" who have a feel for rap, there is a window of opportunity and a possibility of success (however that is measured).

At the same time, rappers, acting as observers and interlocutors, occupy a somewhat contradictory position. If they do well, they offer a model for others to emulate and aspire to, but at the same time material success does not mitigate institutional and systemic racisms that put them under surveillance and hold them in place. As contemporary Black British musical genres, grime and UK drill offer an insight into identity and belonging in an environment that does not acknowledge or recognise the historical reasons for a Black presence. While drawing on familiar aggrandising and materialistic rap tropes, it must be said that the lyrical content also counters lazy stereotypes made about young Black people. When we look and listen beyond the obvious bravado and toughness of the lyrical expression, what emerges is the ways in which artists speak to complex realities, where everyday life includes trauma and pain as well as joy.

Rap, in its many iterations, is a ubiquitous soundscape. Through the production and consumption of rap, grime and UK drill, communities from "ends" have been narrating their everyday reality for decades, articulating how life in the UK takes place in often within the contours of austerity, racism and police brutality.[81] During pandemic time, small acts such as walking or sitting in public, as well as more intentional actions such as going on a protest, were subjected to punitive measures, surveillance and control. With this in mind, it is possible to see how Black popular music provides a unique way of seeing and knowing the world.

CHAPTER 5
MODES OF ENTREPRENEURSHIP IN PANDEMIC TIME

Once lockdown was announced in March 2020, we had no option but to stay at home. And even when we were able to participate in public life again, it had to be at a distance. Like many, I was sat in front of a screen for more hours than usual, for work and entertainment. Spending more time watching television, in the summer of 2021, I caught a glimpse of an advertisement for primary school uniforms. As schools had remained closed for many months in the previous year, this thirty-second commercial gestured towards a return to some kind of normality. The broadcast was for Asda — a UK national supermarket chain — for their own brand of children's clothing.[1] On the face of it, it was standard practice to show commercials for uniform and school supplies at that time of year. What was unusual was its use of a drill beat, and its presentation in the style of a grime music video.

What Asda was doing was tapping into and building on the huge success of the UK drill track "Body" by Russ Millions x Tion Wayne in March 2021, and the subsequent remix in April 2021.[2] Over the previous three years, UK drill had made inroads into the national charts via 2018's "Funky Friday" by Dave (ft Fredo).[3] In June 2019, grime featured as a headline act at a festival for the first time,[4] and in December 2019, East London grime MC D Double E provided the soundtrack for an IKEA Christmas TV advert.[5] Taken together, these events indicate how both genres have come to be embedded in UK mainstream culture as a commodified sonic backdrop to everyday life. As these sounds, as well as their allied entrepreneurial activities, took on an even deeper significance in pandemic time, my starting point is to contextualise the role and place of entrepreneurship in the rap music economy.

Entrepreneurship in Rap

Entrepreneurship is viewed as a process by which an economy as a whole can move forward. It is something that disrupts the equilibrium of the market (through innovation and new combinations) and creates movement. It is therefore assumed to be at the root of economic improvement and the key to economic growth, productivity and the diffusion of knowledge. As entrepreneurs naturally strive for innovation and new ways of doing business, they are seen as a positive force for movement and growth in the economy. There is a correlation between the number of entrepreneurs and the growth rate of the economy; indeed, the creation of new firms is seen as a driving force for economic growth.[6]

What an entrepreneur does is also loosely defined, but, broadly speaking, they seek change and exploit the opportunities that come from that change,[7] are people who find ways to add to their own power and prestige,[8] and also exploit the value of new ideas or carve out new activities.[9] Entrepreneurship therefore lies at the crux of two crucial points: lucrative opportunities and enterprising individuals.[10]

Until fairly recently, the archetypal entrepreneur had a somewhat mythical status; they were not like the rest of us, as they embodied a set of unique characteristics that set them apart.[11] In the age of the internet and social media, however, the impact of technology has altered the meaning of enterprise and entrepreneurial activity, and it now occurs in everyday spaces and places. In a neoliberal context, the monetisation of the side hustle, and indeed the main hustle, takes centre stage.

As economist Jacques Attali points out, "music is an immaterial pleasure that has become a commodity" that cannot be separated from the wider economy.[12] Aside from that, most musicians have to work within the contours of art and the market, where being entrepreneurial is now seen as an essential attribute.[13] In capitalist economies, many musical genres provide a soundtrack to consumer culture, but what separates rap is its willingness and ability to reference brands visually and lyrically.[14]

Key thematic concerns of rap are identity and location.[15] I would add that entrepreneurship is also a primary theme — and for those from the "hood" or the "ends" it is both a politics and an ethics.[16] By that I mean the application of *the hustle* — making the most of meagre resources and adopting a nimble approach to start and sustain an enterprise.

In *Black Noise*, one of the first major academic studies into the cultural and economic significance of rap, sociologist Tricia Rose invites us to think about rap in different ways.[17] Written at a time when rap attracted controversy as degenerate, disturbing "noise" rather than music, Rose outlines how the commercial value of perceived resistance complicates rap's marginality. A key tension exists in rap: as a musical form, it is held in contempt for its perceived lack of musicality, while at the same time it is held in high esteem by a wide and ever-increasing audience. Entrepreneurship within rap has a commercial value that takes it beyond noise. Participating in the rap scene allows people to evolve into different roles and identities — for example, moving from rapper to writer to host to entrepreneur.

Far from operating in a vacuum, entrepreneurship is a social phenomenon anchored within a socio-cultural context.[18] In the US context, in an environment of ever-decreasing opportunities, young people from racially marginalised communities turn to music enterprise as a way to make a living. Creative and entrepreneurial spaces with music at the centre allowed artists to turn "survival culture" responses to poverty and unemployment into musical resources.[19]

Social capital, in terms of concrete resources such as editing skills and production skills, and tangible resources such as feedback, positive regard and appreciation, is gained from working in this sector. Artist/entrepreneurs in the contemporary music economy challenge the accepted notion of the entrepreneur by undertaking activity which is clearly rooted in their social and cultural circumstance and extending that into the wider world. Many of these artist/entrepreneurs are firmly located in their inner-city environs, and therefore economic capital is likely to be scarce.

Once an individual has scanned the horizon and has an awareness of the limits of opportunities that are available, they then draw on their creative and/or technical skills in order to carve out a niche for themselves. Skills can be honed through practice, observation of other "old hands" and mentoring. Individuals also have access to technology, social media and online platforms where they can share their creative output directly with their audience and receive feedback. The contemporary rap music economy creates an environment in which artist/entrepreneurs are able to learn from each other. This is enhanced by accessible communication and social media, which enables a cross-fertilisation of not just creative ideas but business ideas also. Products that are developed include mixtapes — now essentially a collection of tracks for download rather than a physical product — as well as single tracks, associated merchandise and live events.[20]

When few resources are available, being able to pool skills and knowledge means that your track and its accompanying video will be more likely to come to fruition. Multiple actors and stakeholders are involved in the creation and distribution of a piece of work. Artist/entrepreneurs take from and give back to the social realm in terms of material for their creative output and as source of relevant and readily available skills.[21] Grime MCs and drill rappers are an integral part of their social and economic situation, and for the most part these circumstances have less to offer in terms of employment and opportunity. On the whole, participants in this economy learn by doing, or become conversant by watching others and taking their inspiration from them. In the past, young people congregating on council estates, on street corners and in youth clubs led to creative clusters where musical innovation flourished. For drill rappers, the communities and clusters are mainly online, because it has come up in a digital age.[22]

Music as Commodity

As a Black musical form, rap entertains and is enjoyed by millions around the globe. In its various forms, rap resonates with the marginalised and the disadvantaged. In the five decades since its inception, the conditions in which music in general is made have changed significantly. Digital music technologies such as streaming have altered the way consumers access and listen to music. Platforms such as Spotify offer continuous access to an enormous amount of choice.[23] For the artist, the task is to try and capture attention in a very crowded arena, to be able to "cut through the noise of the internet to grab the attention of the audience".[24] Income from streaming — except for a few global superstars — is minimal, and therefore artists rely ever more on live performance and allied merchandise, as well as advertising and sponsorship deals.[25] At the same time, the internet business model — where individuals and organisations can become successful by selling low volumes of niche products — is underpinned by a "techno-optimism" that promises increased access for all within the global creative economy.[26]

Considering music as commodity gives us an insight to other social and economic relations.[27] We can see this in the ways in which UK drill rappers, for example, embody a continuity of entrepreneurial practice, underpinned by the pursuit of "digital clout" in order to raise their online profile and ultimately boost their income.[28] Music offers an illustration of a commodified society, where it simply becomes another commodity and therefore an object from which to extract income.[29] For some rappers, although they can still "use their music to shout their suffering, their dreams of the absolute and freedom",[30] it sometimes comes at a cost to their creative expression or their liberty.[31]

In addition, changes in the music economy and the music industry have increased consumer demand for more and more creative output, and it is this aspect, coupled with an unwillingness to wait for or pay for music, which means that in many respects musicians may face a precarious existence. Indeed, a recent study showed how most musicians do not earn a living wage, and have to develop other income streams to get by.[32] A neoliberal framework supposes that success or failure is the result of individual endeavour. If all is attributed to personal responsibility, what happens if your dream "fails"?

A deeper dive into the contemporary rap music economy reveals a creative practice that mimics neoliberalist endeavours in that it is highly individualised, and yet at the same time adopts a collaborative, borderless approach. It is worth noting that while the push for participation in this sector often comes from economic adversity, there is also a desire to be financially autonomous, creative individuals. In a neoliberal landscape, self-employment and entrepreneurship are seen as routes to material success.[33] However, although it is evident that these entrepreneurs are "buying in to neoliberal capitalism" in an individual attempt to overcome advanced marginality,[34] this effort occurs at the same time as collective endeavour — and the "bring in", or collaborative activity, is a key aspect of this music economy, nationally and internationally. Nevertheless, economic enrichment is a collective enterprise as well as an individual one, and the music scene can offer a valid route to employment,[35] albeit with the caveat that the endless demand from consumers for new product means that in many respects creativity often becomes something akin to a factory production line. At the same time, for musicians and music workers, promoting themselves and being entrepreneurial is now an essential part of the work, as is the making of an individual brand. Beyond the economic exchange, all music-related activities are considered to be work, and this comes with a cost to emotional wellbeing.[36]

Social/Enterprise in Pandemic Time

Drawing on an established sound system enterprise culture, grime music practitioners laid a blueprint for what came after in terms of starting with few resources and having a DIY approach. Another foundational practice was the early adoption of emerging technology and using it in innovative ways. I will focus here on two online responses during the pandemic: a radio station and a series of interviews which formed the basis of a fundraising campaign. At the heart of both events is contemporary Black music.

During pandemic time, an online radio station, No Signal, emerged on May Day 2020. At that time, lockdown had been going on for several weeks, with no clear end in sight. The founders, brothers Jojo and David Sonubi, had a background in organising Black music events, such as day parties and clubnights, but Covid-19 had put an end to that. Beginning as a livestream on Instagram, No Signal initially broadcast online from the presenters' bedrooms. Switching to Google Hangouts to allow more audience interaction, the show quickly gained listeners. One popular theme was NS10v10 — essentially a sound clash — where DJs played ten tunes from two artists pitted against each other. Some of the first shows featured East London rappers Kojo Funds and J Hus, and veteran grime MCs Kano and Dizzee Rascal. Further shows included Burna Boy and Popcaan (Nigerian Afrobeats and Jamaican dancehall respectively).

The show captured the imagination of Black Twitter — a space for creativity, commentary and contribution. Black Twitter is a "Black cultural discourse, it generates conversations that link to a global structure".[37] As an online gathering of users who "identify as Black *and* share Black cultural commonplaces", Black Twitter affects and influences public opinion.[38] On Black Twitter, a multitude of Black cultural identities are expressed through digital practices, and the use of the hashtag raises the visibility of Black cultural discourse. However, as André Brock reminds us, you cannot just show up and take part because "participating in Black Twitter requires a deep knowledge of Black culture, commonplaces, and digital practices".[39]

Twitter Commentary

From BET[40]

Vybz Kartel vs Wizkid   Who y'all got? #NS10v10

• Vybz Kartel
36.8%

• Wizkid
63.2%

80,961 votes·Final results

9:33 PM · May 3, 2020

No Signal is the culture's pandemic champion, which was born during lockdown with their viral #NS10v10 battle which kept us all entertained and took the internet by storm

Can we get another lockdown just so we can go through that #ns10v10 time again

Some people will think of banana bread, Joe Wicks and plants when thinking back on 2020 covid culture. For me, it'll be Ziwe's Instagram interviews, Verzus, D-Nice's #ClubQuarantine and No Signal Radio's #NS10v10 — all of them black creators contributing to culture.

By September, No Signal had expanded the battle concept to include record labels, eras, producers and even locations.[41] Through being amplified on Black Twitter during lockdown, No Signal had attracted national and international attention,[42] and had a mission to "represent the black diaspora as a whole".[43] Post-lockdown, No Signal has evolved into a traditional enterprise, securing partnerships with alcohol companies and streaming services.

By contrast, recording artist, grime MC and actor Kano (Kane Robinson) responded to the isolation and the specific local impact of Covid-19 in Newham by hosting a series of online interviews.[44] All of the guests had a link to the borough in some way. Branded as "Newham Talks" and uploaded and shared via YouTube,[45] he used his reputation, local connections/knowledge and brand to fundraise for local causes.[46] The fundraiser was reported on and discussed in online music platforms and local newspapers, as well as the music press.[47] Twitter commentary was sparse, but on YouTube, roughly half a million people have watched the videos. Full disclosure, I was one of the interviewees of Newham Talks — where, if you watch closely, you can see my previous book on the table.[48] As recording took place in the first few weeks of lockdown, it was quite a surreal experience, as the everyday markers of time passing had been disrupted. It was also one of the first times that I had recorded an interview online. By using memories, music and lived experiences, the interviews contributed to a sense of social connection and belonging at a time when lockdown kept us socially distant from one another. The comments on YouTube under the various interviews reflect a broad audience and indicate an intergenerational divide with younger viewers, who knew Kano only as an actor in *Top Boy*, as well as the realisation that Idris Elba is from East London:

Interview with Idris Elba (actor, *The Wire*, *Luther*, *Mandela*)

Love it, Idris talking about Stringer Bell to Kano, who plays Sully, both actors elevated these characters in their respective shows.

I know him as kano but my old man only knew him as sully until I told him enjoyed this a lot both of them interesting to listen to.

Interview with Ghetts (grime MC, recording artist)

Having grown up in hackney and Waltham forest, i gotta say, ghetts is 100% right when it comes to the level of musical talent coming out of newham, unrivalled. Ghetts even missed a few names. Imagine the festival you could have. Shame the roads do this!!! This was a good listen from 2 greats.

Aww bless, love the cameraderie [sic] between these two.

Coming from Newham myself, I found this truly inspirational and beautiful. Although we all love the ends, the aim is to get out of it like these two did. I wish the young generation from Newham would take a thing or two from these great legends.

Interview with Christine Ohuruogu (Olympic athlete)

Well done Kano! Your tone of voice is inviting and chill. Looking forward to seeing more. Great chat!! I always rooted for Christine. Best of Team GB.

"Something in the water" would be a great title project for a collaborative album regrouping all Newham MCs and artists, or more generally for a podcast on East London's contribution to the arts and culture.

Music as Community

Prior to the pandemic, we had become accustomed to a hyper-individualised neoliberal landscape imbued with an "organised loneliness".[49] Increased individualisation coupled with the decimation of public space means fewer opportunities for people to come together. Pandemic time heightened these feelings of loneliness and isolation, and blurred boundaries between life online and offline.

During the lockdown period, Kano, steeped in a DIY, grime tradition, draws on its business practices and entrepreneurial spirit to fundraise for social enterprises for the area he grew up in. At the same time, the organisers of No Signal radio used their existing skills and networks to take their events online. Connecting with a wider listenership via Black Twitter, No Signal entertained an international audience. Experiencing radio online allowed listeners to participate in an imagined "mediated liveness" and share a feeling of co-presence. In a period of lockdown and social isolation, being in a "live" online community offered ways to mark time, create meaning, and share positive experiences.[50]

What rap music provides, in all its forms, is a means of expression, a possibility of visibility and success. The economy which it forms a part of includes identity, belonging and enterprise at its heart. Those who do become successful (however that is measured) have a unique opportunity to foster social connection. Bear in mind, though, that street culture, when inhabited and occupied by Black youth, becomes attached and applied to violent modes of behaviour.[51] Recent iterations of rap such as grime and UK drill have been seen as contributing to the pull of "road life" and its inherent criminal acts.[52] In this way, some Black modes of creative expression may become a trap, as they can create a route to contain young people from marginalised communities. It plays into the idea that success can only be achieved through the adoption of a violent criminal persona.[53] And of course, for Black youth, regardless of whether or not they are grime MCs or drill rappers, the costs and consequences can be dire.

Joint enterprise, lengthy prison sentences, deportation and displacement are all in play here.[54]

For young people from "ends" using music as a possible way out, there is an existential crisis if the exit does not happen. Also, popularity and visibility through music might mean coming under the view of the regulating authorities, and for some this may lead to a more precarious position. At the same time, through enterprise and enterprising activities in the contemporary Black British music economy, young Black women and men — marginalisation notwithstanding — are drawing on a continuity of practice to create meaningful work for themselves and others. And having something to do is key, because if one is *doing* something, then it opens up the possibility of *being* something. Participation allows young people to keep out of trouble. But it is much more than that. Grime artists and drill rappers have used music to articulate the nature of their living conditions, to speak of the lack of opportunity and at the same time create a route to employment in the creative and cultural industries — sectors which continue to be an exclusive, white and middle-class enclave.[55]

Contradictions arise, however, with the possibility of material success and individual liberation that take the artists away from the people that they ostensibly represent. In other ways, institutions and systems operate in such a way that, despite success, the artist never quite escapes the "hood". And this can be seen in the application of surveillance mechanisms, policing and control which hold the rapper in place.[56] Grime and UK drill are contemporary examples of Black sound as a continuing cause for concern.[57] At the same time, the sound, lyrics, the aesthetic and the enterprising activities make connections beyond national borders. Even if corporations extract from and dilute it, rap in all its forms still belongs and speaks to marginal racialised communities. Rappers can use their profile to speak to the everyday struggles of ordinary people's lives and point to a way out, on, or up. Music offers a space for play and care, as well as a sense of achievement and belonging, factors which often get lost in the problematising lens that is applied to contemporary Black British musical forms. The artist/entrepreneurs who are the core of this sector are working for love and money. We can see how young men and women have used their creative practice to uncover a different way of being in the world. In so doing, despite the material and physical constraints of pandemic time, social connection and social action become real prospects.

Conclusion

Today, entrepreneurship is deemed to be common sense, a force for good that sparks innovation and leads to progress. However, in Western economies, inequality is baked in, and entrepreneurship does not necessarily erode the gap between rich and poor. During the pandemic, while many people lost income and struggled to get by, a recent Oxfam report showed how the top ten richest men doubled their income.[58] Narratives regarding entrepreneurship also feature heavily in the contemporary music industry, reflecting general shifts in the wider economy. On the whole, musicians have become entrepreneurial by necessity as advances in digital technology have radically changed the sector.[59]

Musicians were among the first to have their working lives and income challenged by digital media. As a result, they quickly adapted by using the internet and social media to build relationships. Engaging with digital technology as a hope for sustainable income in the future,[60] musicians use social media to interact directly with fans. A digital marketplace where music and its by-products can be bought and sold offers a possibility to generate income. In such a landscape, musicians become content providers, jostling for attention amongst podcasters, audiobooks and crime documentaries. However, as well as the financial stresses that are now commonplace in the sector, there is also the perpetual struggle between creativity and commerce.[61]

It is worth making the point that technology and its advances have to be viewed within the context of late-stage capitalism, where all of life is commodified. During pandemic time, those that could worked from home, and the work of musicians (in a number of formats) kept us entertained. But behind the curtain of accessible, freeing technology lies precarity, exploitation and ill health.[62] Technology was supposed to free us. Far from democratising the process through which music is shared and financially rewarded, technology firms continue to increase their power and act as gatekeepers to the music industry.[63] Aside from that, particular musical forms such as grime or drill have become a surveillance tool in many ways, and young Black people are all too easily caught up in the most punitive aspects of state control.

In the rap music economy, entrepreneurship encompasses a DIY ethic and is a driver to amass individual wealth; it operates as part of everyday logics and practice. That being said, and taking collective endeavours into account, entrepreneurship and individual philanthropy are not a replacement for social investment.

CONCLUSION
IT'S NOT OVER YET...

Faded "Keep your distance" sign, September 2023

At the time of writing, the Covid-19 Inquiry in the UK is ongoing.[1] Interventions during the pandemic to limit the spread of the virus mapped onto existing societal inequalities, so although we had similar experiences, we were not all affected in the same way. Clearly, we were not "all in it together" if billionaires increased their profits at the same time that "the most disadvantaged in Britain are no better off than 15 years ago".[2] Covid-19 continues to have an impact on many lives, and we are only just starting to hear the full extent of the consequences of the UK government's response to the pandemic. Each day, reports from the inquiry let us know how some lives and social groups were deemed to be disposable. Thinking through those weeks and months when people died alone, away from their families and friends, and when numbers at funerals were restricted, is a momentous task. Maybe it is too soon to reflect on a period of time that for many people had a negative psychological impact, an abrupt interruption loaded with frustration, boredom, financial loss and fear.

Since December 2021, social and economic life has opened up, but it is against a backdrop of the long-lasting psychological effects of lockdown, as well as higher levels of physical and mental ill health.[3] How social life is organised has changed since pandemic time. Online options have become the norm. We have become more used to the idea of being a "digital audience" in our cultural experiences, which has benefits (for example in terms of accessibility) as well as limitations.[4]

During pandemic time, popular culture took on an even more profound significance, "preserving a sense of life being lived", particularly when venues had to close down and we were confined to our homes.[5] Contemporary Black music, the focus of this book, provided a way to keep us connected in a multitude of ways. The value of popular culture is often ignored and its content misunderstood. Aesthetic tastes and division between high and low culture draw upon and reinforce patterns of social inequalities. The cultural capital of the dominant classes ensured that opera and theatre were supported and protected early on in the pandemic, whereas popular music did not receive the same attention or intervention until much later.[6]

My goal with this book was to focus on a window in time — March 2020 to December 2021 — a period of nearly two years when life was interrupted and reconfigured. Taking into consideration the UK government response to the pandemic, we can see that a collapse in long-term thinking and planning meant that the UK was badly affected, with a high number of cases and as well as high death count. Mitigations put in place to prevent the spread of Covid-19 included lockdown, social distancing and travel restrictions, measures which had a significant socio-economic impact. Businesses in every sector had to adapt quickly, and although support from government for the music industry came eventually, it was later than for other sectors. For those who were already in a precarious position, the financial consequences were dire. As many aspects of life moved online, we consumed music in various formats, and sonic events offered much-needed social connection.

The global pandemic served as an interruption in time, a serious crisis that revealed stark social and economic inequalities. Contemporary neoliberal capitalism has always employed division and injustice in terms of how work is rewarded and valued,[7] but Covid-19 made it impossible to ignore the economic chasm in the everyday lives of the well-off and of those on low incomes. As a society, we relied on the essential work of poorly paid workers, often on precarious employment contracts. *Build Back Fairer: The Covid-19 Marmot Review* highlighted how austerity had stalled growth in life expectancy and pointed out the ways in which Covid-19 disproportionately affected those on low income and racialised minorities.[8] While some may wish to move on from where we are, it's not over yet. We have yet to see whether, in the aftermath of a global pandemic, underpinned by more than a decade of austerity that hollowed out and outsourced public services, there is a shift in political consciousness or an ideological commitment to a fairer society.

Late-stage, neoliberal capitalism locates us in "liquid times" — an age of uncertainty where social forms do not keep their shape for long, where the state contracts out its functions to private enterprise, and "communal state endorsed insurance against individual failure and ill fortune" has gradually been withdrawn.[9] Social structures had been weakened by neoliberalism and austerity, and yet we were supposed to pull together in pandemic time. In the early days of the pandemic, fear and hyper-individualism saw people clearing supermarket shelves and hoarding goods. As we moved through the following weeks and months, mutual aid efforts made an appearance, and we looked for ways to connect to each other.

Pandemic time moved along without the usual everyday markers, and left us with shapeless spaces to fill. Music in this context, takes on a more significant role as a "technology of the self" — as a way to remember who we were as well as be in community with others. The challenge has been in trying to document a time that is still unfolding, attempting to make sense of an era that is simultaneously past and present.

Music was a source of light-heartedness and joy; in times of uncertainty and isolation, it provided a connection to sociality. I have focused on an eclectic selection of sonic events to articulate how we used contemporary Black musical expression to pass the time in pandemic time. From the viral online #DontRushChallenge to the sound of applause as we clapped for the NHS, we sought ways to break the pervasive muffling of everyday life.

Musicking works as an in-person activity; however, in pandemic time, it meant taking part online in musical performance, listening, commenting and providing content. Through the *Verzuz* battles on social media, we witnessed Beenie Man and Bounty Killa bring the dancehall clash — reworked for the constraints of the pandemic — to a wider audience. The *Small Axe* anthology series broadcast a film — with lovers rock music as a soundtrack — to a locked-in, intergenerational audience. Finally, when we were allowed back outside — albeit in a restricted way — I took part in an in-person music event at the Southbank, but with no singing, no dancing and having to remain seated.

Thinking through how sonic Black geographies provide a sense of place, connection and belonging allows a consideration of rappers as observers, interlocutors and social commentators. Through a Black Atlantic lens, we can see how rap in all its forms has become a significant cultural force. It speaks to and for the social, economic and political concerns of marginalised communities. Entrepreneurship is an intrinsic part of the rap lexicon, and enterprise takes on different modes during pandemic time. The "clash" format that is a staple of Jamaican sound system culture is reworked by No Signal for an online, locked-in audience. Boosted by Black Twitter, No Signal's 10v10 battles flourish internationally. Also online, rapper/actor Kano used social media in an enterprising way to raise funds for local causes. As well as donations, online commentary allows an intergenerational audience to feel that they are part of something beyond their immediate surroundings.

In this book, under the broad term of "Black popular culture", I have looked at a number of musical forms: lovers rock, dancehall, rap, grime and UK drill. I have focused on musical affiliations and connections across time and space. The book also serves as a way to reflect on passing time musically in a pandemic, hopefully unlocking social memories that will allow us to explore what it means to be human when the texture of life suddenly unravels, specifically in the context of separation, isolation and daily death tolls.

Black musical expression during pandemic time was a salve that went beyond invoking a sense of belonging and acting as a counter to isolation. Historically, as Paul Gilroy reminds us, "Black musics have provided a precious means of healing and recovery".[10] What is maybe muted or less explicit in the musical accounts that are the focus of this book is "the traditional Black Atlantic culture of dissent",[11] so I have attempted to show the ways in which these musical forms might also articulate perspectives that offered more than just entertainment.

Signs for social distancing may have faded, but it's not over yet. Our social, economic and cultural lives were transformed during an interruption in time. Whether the residue of pandemic time leads to a fairer society is an open question. Nevertheless, we cannot "go back to normal" if normality meant unfairness, inequality and injustice. But in many ways, we did. When social restrictions came to an end, society reconfigured around old patterns and norms. However, there were some changes for the better. And as I come to the end of this book, I see glimmers of hope. Work patterns became more flexible for some, and for those that were able to, working from home became a new norm. Also, there has been a resurgence in the fight for better pay and working conditions, and a renewed willingness to take industrial action to achieve this — nurses, doctors, teachers, postal workers and train drivers withdrew their labour, often with the support of the general public. Maybe there has been a reawakening to the fact that the workers society needed the most were valued the least in monetary terms. Perhaps we recognised that for a liveable life we need to invest in public services. After all, these are the services that we needed the most. We should all be striving for what David Hesmondhalgh and Sarah Baker called simply "good work"[12] — in other words, work that is meaningful and that allows us to flourish rather than just exist. For musicians, there is an additional layer to the work: as well as making a living, the task is to relate to an audience, to encourage those connections that help us to "hold onto our basic humanity".[13]

Engaging with musical forms of popular culture allows us to understand and contest wider social structures and power relations, particularly at a time when economic growth is deemed to be the all-important element to better living conditions, and less attention is paid the consequences of pursuing infinite economic expansion. Studying the rituals and practice of everyday life also offers the possibility for a radical reimagining of how things could be —maybe of a better world. As Corey Miles reminds us, "interrogating popular culture allows us to dig a little deeper" and come to some understanding of how music gives context to feelings, social relationships and environment.[14]

Towards the end of the time period for this book, in December 2021, I was interviewed for the podcast *Xconversation*.[15] Socially distanced, it was recorded in a repurposed shipping container in Bow, East London. The hosts were two young Black men with lived experience of the criminal justice system. Both had served long prison sentences. In our discussion prior to the recording, as we were warming up, we spoke about music. We had a nourishing, intergenerational conversation that took us across time and space. The hosts talked about being locked up in a cell for hours at a time and the difference that music made — as a link to home, as a connection to others.[16] Music kept them going — it was an anchor, a site for memories and feelings; it was something to hold on to. It gave them something to talk about beyond those four walls. Taking part in that conversation and watching the interview with grime MC Scorcher (who has also spent time in prison) on YouTube later,[17] I was struck by the care in the everyday practice of sharing words and feelings with a wider world.

I raise this here as an illustration of an everyday reimagining of a better world, even during pandemic time. Music and lyrics are methods with which tell a story, get a message across and make human connections. A preoccupation with nihilistic lyrics means that we miss hearing and seeing some musical genres as a response to socio-economic conditions — and, in a hyper-capitalist neoliberal economy, to put it bluntly, it sells. So there are benefits, for some, to performing an excised, dislocated "Blackness" that presents an aesthetic without meaning.

In this context, *Xconversation*'s podcast exists as a radical act of care, the public face of the work it does in the community. In addition, organisations such as Healing Justice in London[18] and the MAIA group in Birmingham[19] challenge existing structures and aim to dismantle cycles of harm. These bold, collective responses in a hyper-individualised world remind us that our communities can be rebuilt with care. From these everyday activities the world can change. The work these organisations and many like them are doing forces us to rethink the life-limiting treadmill of never-ending work. Carving out spaces for reflection, healing and care that counter, in some ways, the organised loneliness of a neoliberal landscape offers a glimpse into a radically reimagined future.

NOTES

Introduction/Interruption

1   Hall, S., 1996. "What is this 'Black' in Black Cultural Studies?",
    in Chen, K.H. and Morley, D. (eds) *Stuart Hall: Critical
    Dialogues in Cultural Studies*. (London: Routledge), pp. 468–
    478, p. 469.

2   Ibid., p. 470.

3   Gilroy, P., 1993. *Small Acts: Thoughts on the Politics of Black
    Cultures* (London: Serpent's Tail), p. 256.

4   Chen, K.H. and Morley, D. (eds), 2006. *Stuart Hall: Critical
    Dialogues in Cultural Studies*. (London: Routledge), p. 443.

5   Ibid., p. 448.

6   Gilroy, P., 2020. "Vexed History: Time and the Waning
    of Heart-I-Cal Philosophy", in *Narratives from Beyond the
    UK Reggae Bassline: The System is Sound* (Cham: Springer
    International Publishing), pp. 7–28, p. 10.

7   Spence, K.M., 2021. "Caribbean Creatives and the Intelligent
    Economy", in *Intelligent Economies: Developments in the
    Caribbean* (California: Informing Science Press), pp. 145–186.

8   This sonic landscape heavily featured Burna Boy — *Last, Last*
    and Pheelz, *Finesse* (ft Bnxn) and the Dancehall version from
    Ding Dong — now reworked as *Happiness*. See Burna Boy -
    Last Last, https://www.youtube.com/watch?v=421w1j87fEM;
    Pheelz - Finesse (ft. BNXN), https://youtu.be/
    Vcwhe0pY4Bg?si=rSP6lLYqQJw3SsS5; Ding Dong - Happiness,
    https://youtu.be/BSSDscMW6Yw?si=wwTy4XHxCaNSBcqq

9   Massey, D., 2000. "Travelling Thoughts", in *Without Guarantees: In Honour of Stuart Hall* (London: Verso), pp. 225–232.

10 Gilroy, P. "Vexed History", p. 9.

11 See also White, J. & Ilan, J., 2020. "Ethnographer Soundclash: A UK Rap and Grime Story". *Riffs*, 2021: Volume 5, Issue 2.

12 Du Gay P., 2000. "Representing 'Globalization': Notes on the Discursive Orderings of Economic Life", in *Without Guarantees: In Honour of Stuart Hall*, pp. 113–125.

13 Anderson, B., 2006. *Imagined Communities: Reflections on the Origin and Spread of Nationalism* (London: Verso).

Chapter 1: A Window in Time

1   Message from 10 Downing St, 24 March 2020, https://www.youtube.com/watch?v=u4Zz6UcOVbE

2   "Prime Minister's statement on coronavirus (COVID-19)", 12 March 2020, https://www.gov.uk/government/speeches/pm-statement-on-coronavirus-12-march-2020

3   Tang, J.W. et al., 2022. "An Exploration of the Political, Social, Economic and Cultural Factors Affecting How Different Global Regions Initially Reacted to the COVID-19 Pandemic". *Interface Focus*, 12(2), p. 202.

4   "Covid-19: Italy confirms 11 deaths as cases spread from north". *BMJ*, 2020;368:m757.

5   In March 2020, a headline appeared in the *Guardian*: "Italians sang out in solidarity during a nationwide lockdown", https://www.youtube.com/watch?v=Q734VN0N7hw

6   In March 2020, *Politico* compared Covid-19 lockdown measures in the EU and the UK. Only Sweden had no lockdown, although non-essential travel was banned and all public events were cancelled, https://www.politico.eu/article/europes-coronavirus-lockdown-measures-compared/

7   The *Guardian* reported on 11 January 2020, "First death from China mystery illness outbreak", https://www.theguardian.

com/world/2020/jan/11/china-mystery-illness-outbreak-causes-first-death

8   Chen, M.H. et al., 2020. "The Impact of Policy Responses to COVID-19 on US Travel and Leisure Companies". *Annals of Tourism Research Empirical Insights*, 1(1), p. 100003.

9   Shubhadeep, R. et al., 2020. "Viral Pandemics of the Last Four Decades: Pathophysiology, Health Impacts and Perspectives". *International Journal of Environmental Research and Public Health*, 2020 Dec; 17(24), p. 9411, https://www.ncbi.nlm.nih.gov/pmc/articles/PMC7765415/#:~:text=These%20include%20the%20Human%20Immunodeficiency,Syndrome%20Coronavirus%2D2%20(SARS%2D

10 Williams, S.N. et al., 2020. "Public Perceptions and Experiences of Social Distancing and Social Isolation During the COVID-19 Pandemic: A UK-Based Focus Group Study". *BMJ*, 10(7), p. e039334.

11 Wilson, B., 2020. "Off Our Trolleys: What Stockpiling in the Coronavirus Crisis Reveals About Us". *Guardian*, 3 April 2020, https://www.theguardian.com/news/2020/apr/03/off-our-trolleys-what-stockpiling-in-the-coronavirus-crisis-reveals-about-us

12 See ITV news report, "UK retailers urge shoppers to 'be considerate' amid coronavirus panic buying", https://www.youtube.com/watch?v=rLbPSb7d18M

13 Holt, L. and Murray, L., 2022. "Children and Covid-19 in the UK". *Children's Geographies*, 20(4), pp. 487–494.

14 Some Scandinavian countries (Norway, Finland, Denmark and Iceland) and Central and Eastern European countries (Hungary, Slovakia, the Czech Republic, Romania, Poland, Bulgaria and Ukraine) also managed to control the virus well, reporting fewer than five hundred new cases per day. See Tang, J.W., "An Exploration of the Political, Social, Economic and Cultural Factors Affecting How Different Global Regions Initially Reacted to the COVID-19 Pandemic".

15 Research published in 2021 which looked at Ghana, Guinea, Liberia, Niger, Nigeria and Sierra Leone showed that although the effects on mortality were less, there are huge social consequences for vulnerable populations. See Saalim, K. et al., 2021. "Reported health and social consequences of the COVID-19 pandemic on vulnerable populations and implemented solutions in six West African countries: A media content analysis". *Plos One*, 16(6), p. e0252890.

16 Rosenthal, P.J. et al., 2020. "COVID-19: Shining the Light on Africa". *The American Journal of Tropical Medicine and Hygiene*, 102(6), p. 1145 shows how African countries responded quickly to the challenges of the Covid-19 pandemic, implementing a number of measures thorough the setting up of a taskforce (Africa Taskforce for the Coronavirus Preparedness).

17 The African Development Bank predicts an estimated loss of twenty million jobs across the continent due to the pandemic. See Rosenthal, P.J. et al., "COVID-19: Shining the Light on Africa", p. 1145.

18 Tang, J.W. "An Exploration of the Political, Social, Economic and Cultural Factors Affecting How Different Global Regions Initially Reacted to the COVID-19 Pandemic".

19 Ibid.

20 Jamaica is the "Birthplace of 6 distinct musical genres: mento, ska, reggae, rocksteady, dub and dancehall. Kingston, the capital has been a UNESCO Music City since 2015", https://citiesofmusic.net/city/kingston/

21 Jamaica documented 44,337 cases and 744 deaths. See Vasciannie, L.A., 2021. "Jamaica and Covid-19: Issues of Law and Policy in the First Year". *The Round Table*, 110(4), pp. 477–491.

22 Ibid.

23 Tang, J.W. et al. "An Exploration of the Political, Social, Economic and Cultural Factors Affecting How Different Global Regions Initially Reacted to the COVID-19 Pandemic".

24 Holt, L. and Murray, L. "Children and Covid 19 in the UK".

25 Ibid.

26 See "Christmas rules 2020: What are the new rules on mixing?". *BBC News*, 23 December 2020, https://www.bbc.co.uk/news/explainers-55056375

27 "Timeline of UK government coronavirus lockdowns and measures, March 2020 to December 2021", https://www.instituteforgovernment.org.uk/sites/default/files/2022-12/timeline-coronavirus-lockdown-december-2021.pdf

28 "Experts call for inquiry into local death toll after Cheltenham Festival". *Guardian*, 21 April 2020, https://www.theguardian.com/sport/2020/apr/21/experts-inquiry-cheltenham-festival-coronavirus-deaths

29 "Update about Coronavirus (Covid-19): Temporary mortuary facilities to be built on land owned by the City of London Corporation on Wanstead Flats in Manor Park", https://www.newham.gov.uk/news/article/338/update-about-coronavirus-covid-19-temporary-mortuary-facilities-to-be-built-on-land-owned-by-the-city-of-london-corporation-on-wanstead-flats-in-manor-park-from-mayor-rokhsana-fiaz-31-march-2020

30 Morrison, S. "Temporary mortuary in London for 1,300 bodies 'sobering reminder' of coronavirus impact", *Evening Standard*, 14 January 2021, https://www.standard.co.uk/news/health/temporary-london-mortuary-bodies-coronavirus-impact-b899812.html

31 Converting concert and conference facilities, Nightingale hospitals were set up at seven sites across the country, including in London, Birmingham, Harrogate and Manchester. The purpose was to provide critical care facilities. Day, M., 2020. "Covid-19: Nightingale Hospitals Set to Shut Down After Seeing Few Patients". *BMJ*, 2020;369:m1860, https://www.bmj.com/content/369/bmj.m1860

32 Quinn, B. "What has happened to England's seven Nightingale hospitals?". *Guardian*, 8 October 2020, https://www.

theguardian.com/society/2020/oct/08/what-has-happened-to-englands-seven-nightingale-hospitals

33 Roach, A. "Rita Ora apologises and pays £10,000 fine for 'breaking rules' to celebrate 30th birthday". *Evening Standard*, 30 November 2020, https://www.standard.co.uk/news/uk/rita-ora-apologies-lockdown-breach-birthday-instagram-b116454.html

34 "Harlesden street party of 500 people broken up by police". *BBC News*, 3 June 2020, https://www.bbc.co.uk/news/uk-england-london-52902984.

35 "Coronavirus: More than 70 Birmingham parties disrupted by police". *BBC News*, 23 August 2020, https://www.bbc.co.uk/news/uk-england-birmingham-53875805

36 A tier system for local neighbourhoods across the country was put in place so that people could find out which tier they were in, but it was so complicated that the site for the postcode checker crashed, https://gds.blog.gov.uk/2022/07/25/2-years-of-covid-19-on-gov-uk/

37 A support bubble was a network that linked two households — it allowed contact without a need to maintain social distance measures, https://www.gov.uk/guidance/making-a-support-bubble-with-another-household#:~:text=A%20support%20bubble%20is%20a,can%20form%20a%20support%20bubble

38 "Research Briefing — Coronavirus: A History of English Lockdown Laws", 22 December 2021, https://commonslibrary.parliament.uk/research-briefings/cbp-9068/

39 Chen, M.H. et al. "The Impact of Policy Responses to COVID-19 on US Travel and Leisure Companies".

40 Ibid.

41 Nicola, M. et al., 2020. "The Socio-Economic Implications of the Coronavirus Pandemic (COVID-19): A Review". *International Journal of Surgery*, 78, pp. 185–193.

42 Ibid.

43 Coronavirus Job Retention: HMRC would cover 80% of a furloughed employee's wages, up to £2,500 per month. Initially

due to end in May 2020, it ran until September 2021, https://commonslibrary.parliament.uk/the-furlough-scheme-one-year-on/

44 Nicola, M. et al. "The Socio-Economic Implications of the Coronavirus Pandemic (COVID-19)".

45 Williams, S.N. et al. "Public Perceptions and Experiences of Social Distancing and Social Isolation During the COVID-19 Pandemic".

46 Dyer, C., 2022. "Covid-19: Policy to discharge vulnerable patients to care homes was irrational, say judges". *BMJ*, 377, https://doi.org/10.1136/bmj.o1098

47 McKinlay, A.R. et al., 2022. "'You're just there, alone in your room with your thoughts': A qualitative study about the psychosocial impact of the COVID-19 pandemic among young people living in the UK". *BMJ open*, 12(2), p. e053676.

48 Ibid.

49 Holt, L. and Murray, L. "Children and Covid 19 in the UK".

50 McKinlay, A.R. et al. "'You're just there, alone in your room with your thoughts'". From March 2020 to January 2021, Young Minds carried out a series of surveys. They found that for young people with existing mental health issues, the impact of social isolation and loss of everyday routine exacerbated feelings of anxiety and led to a loss of coping mechanisms. Many struggled to cope with the return to secondary school. See "The impact of Covid-19 on young people with mental health needs", https://www.youngminds.org.uk/about-us/reports-and-impact/coronavirus-impact-on-young-people-with-mental-health-needs/

51 McKinlay, A.R. et al. "'You're just there, alone in your room with your thoughts'", p. 1.

52 From 30 March 2020, there were daily press conferences providing updates on the spread of the disease and the measures to contain it. By September, the bulletins had reduced to every few days, ending on 22 February 2022. Slides and datasets for each press conference can be found here:

https://www.gov.uk/government/collections/slides-and-datasets-to-accompany-coronavirus-press-conferences

53 McKinlay, A.R. et al. "'You're just there, alone in your room with your thoughts'".

54 Davies, W., Jai Dutta, S. and Taylor, N., 2022. *Unprecedented?: How Coronavirus Exposed the Politics of Our Economy* (London: Goldsmiths Press), p. 320.

55 McKinlay, A.R. et al. "'You're just there, alone in your room with your thoughts'".

56 Holt, L. and Murray, L. "Children and Covid 19 in the UK".

57 See "Policing the Pandemic in England and Wales: Police use of Fixed Penalty Notices from 27 March 2020 to 31 May 2021", https://blogs.ed.ac.uk/edinburghlawschool/wp-content/uploads/sites/8261/2023/03/NPCC-Report-March-2023-final-1.pdf Key Findings: Between 27 March 2020 and 31 May 2021 police officers in England and Wales issued 122,506 Fixed Penalty Notices FPNs (110,502 in England and 12,004 in Wales) in relation to breaches of restrictions on movement, attending gatherings, and failure to comply with instructions [p. 11]. Almost half of those who received FPNs were aged between 18 and 24 [p. 11]. Over a quarter (27.0%) of FPN recipients in England were from an ethnic minority background, which was around double their population share [p. 12]. In England, the rate of FPNs per 10,000 people from an ethnic minority background was 46.1, compared to 19.9 for white individuals, reflecting an ethnic disparity rate of 2.3. The ethnic disparity rate in England was highest for people from a black ethnic background [p. 12], and for those who were living in areas that were ranked amongst the most deprived in England and Wales [p. 13].

58 Mishra, V. et al., 2021. "Health Inequalities During COVID-19 and their Effects on Morbidity and Mortality". *Journal of Healthcare Leadership*, pp. 19–26.

59 Holt, L. and Murray, L. "Children and Covid 19 in the UK" and Raval, A. "Inside the 'Covid Triangle': A catastrophe years

in the making". *Financial Times*, 5 March 2021, https://www.ft.com/content/0e63541a-8b6d-4bec-8b59-b391bf44a492

60 Rozbicka, P. and Conroy, M. "Live Music and Brexit's Cliffhanger". *Music Business Journal*, Volume 13, Issue 1, https://publications.aston.ac.uk/id/eprint/30302/2/Live_music_and_Brexit_s_cliffhanger.pdf

61 Ibid.

62 Covid-19 and the Music Industry: https://www.icmp.ac.uk/blog/covid-19-and-music-industry

63 Khlystova, O., Kalyuzhnova, Y. and Belitski, M., 2022. "The Impact of the COVID-19 Pandemic on the Creative Industries: A Literature Review and Future Research Agenda". *Journal of Business Research*, 139, pp. 1192–1210.

64 Fraser, T., Crooke, A.H.D. and Davidson, J.W., 2021. "'Music Has No Borders': An Exploratory Study of Audience Engagement With YouTube Music Broadcasts During COVID-19 Lockdown, 2020". *Frontiers in Psychology*, 12, p. 643893.

65 Khlystova, O., Kalyuzhnova, Y. and Belitski, M. "The Impact of the COVID-19 Pandemic on the Creative Industries".

66 Ibid.

67 White, J., 2016. *Urban Music and Entrepreneurship: Beats, Rhymes and Young People's Enterprise*. (Abingdon: Routledge).

68 Howard, F. et al., 2021. "'It's Turned Me from a Professional to a "Bedroom DJ" Once Again': COVID-19 and New Forms of Inequality for Young Music-Makers". *Young*, 29(4), pp. 417–432. This article analysed the impact of the pandemic on young musicians in Australia, England and Portugal.

69 Ntounis, N. et al., 2022. "Tourism and Hospitality Industry Resilience During the Covid-19 Pandemic: Evidence from England". *Current Issues in Tourism*, 25(1), pp. 46–59.

70 Data from Khomami, M. and Sweney, M. "More than a third of UK music industry workers lost jobs in 2020". *Guardian*, 19 October 2021, https://www.theguardian.com/business/2021/oct/19/more-than-a-third-of-uk-music-industry-workers-lost-jobs-2020-covid

71 Sweney, M. "UK music festivals face cancellation without government support". *Guardian*, 5 January 2021, https://www.theguardian.com/music/2021/jan/05/uk-music-festivals-face-cancellation-without-government-support-insurance-coronavirus

72 However, it was not until August 2021 that the government introduced the Live Events Reinsurance Scheme, a cost indemnification insurance scheme to insure against the cancellation, postponement, relocation or abandonment of events due to Covid-19 restrictions. https://www.gov.uk/government/publications/live-events-reinsurance-scheme

73 In July 2020, Oliver Dowden, the Culture Secretary, announced the launch of Film and TV Production Restart Scheme — half a billion pounds for domestic film and TV productions to get support if future losses are incurred due to Covid-19. The Culture Recovery Fund also provided grants to arts organisations. https://www.gov.uk/government/news/dowden-jump-start-for-uks-leading-creative-industries

Chapter 2: Playing with Time — Chronos and Kairos

1 Gagatsis, A. and Gillies, R., 2021. "The Signifier of Time: Music and Sound as Public Utility during the COVID-19 Pandemic". *Musicology Research Journal*, https://research.manchester.ac.uk/en/publications/the-signifier-of-time-music-and-sound-as-public-utility-during-th

2 DeNora, T., 1999. "Music as a Technology of the Self". *Poetics*, 27(1), pp. 31–56, p. 37.

3 See Part 1 in Foucault, M., 2013. *The Archaeology of Knowledge* (London: Routledge).

4 Usually, the clock synchronises our activities as "each of us confronts time in idiosyncratic ways". "Passengerhood" as an organising principle of our sense of time and space. Marder, M., 2022. *Philosophy for Passengers* (Cambridge: MIT Press), p. 56.

5   Ibid., p. 57.

6   Taking place in the UK from 26 March to 28 May, the applause event was unofficial — not government-led. It was influenced by similar gestures in Europe. It was intended to show gratitude for NHS and care workers. Initially, it generated a sense of community for those who took part, but, over time, tensions arose about the purpose of the applause. As the weeks passed, debates about what the applause was for became increasingly complex and divisive. Some felt it was hypocritical to clap for a service that had been underfunded and under-resourced for years. Clapping at the same time as images and news reports circulated of NHS and care workers without adequate PPE infuriated some. See Gagatsis, A. and Gillies, R. "The Signifier of Time", p. 12.

7   Ibid., p. 11.

8   Michael Marder reminds us passengers may be divided into two groups: 1) those that strive to pass the time, 2) those that make time for sundry pursuits, and that "armed with a whole arsenal of recording technologies, we make memories for ourselves", Marder, M., *Philosophy for Passengers*, p. 61.

9   Everett, A., 2009. *Digital Diaspora: A Race for Cyberspace*. (New York: State University of New York Press).

10 Brock Jr, A., 2020. *Distributed Blackness* (New York: New York University Press). Brock's critical technological discourse analysis (CTDA) analyses Black digital life across websites platforms and services. He argues that "digital practitioners filter their technology use through their cultural identity", p. 2. Brock further contends that he wants to "allow Black folk — inescapably connected to the concept of race in the west — to define themselves, in their own voices, as members of a multitudinous culture without being reduced to the political or historical positions proffered by academics", p. 12.

11 Ibid., p. 1.

12 Ibid., p. 218.

13 Ibid.

14 Ibid., p. 219.

15 Ibid., p. 219.

16 Rose, T., 1994. *Black Noise: Rap Music and Black Culture in Contemporary America*. (Hanover, NH: Wesleyan University Press).

17 See *Global Hip Hop Studies*, Volume 2, 2023, https://doi.org/10.1386/ghhs_00041_2. A special issue focusing on hip-hop in Palestine, South Africa, the United States and India.

18 Don't Rush - #StayHome with The OITNB family | #OrangeForever https://www.youtube.com/watch?v=efRJCuXYByk

19 #DontRush challenge from British-African NHS doctors fighting Covid-19, *BBC Africa*, https://www.youtube.com/watch?v=z9ix84YOTyo; *BBC News* item reporting on the Don't Rush challenge by doctors who are from African backgrounds and say they want to challenge the "underrepresentation of diversity in the NHS"; Black medics nail the "NHS Don't Rush" challenge, https://metro.co.uk/video/black-medics-nail-nhs-dont-rush-challenge-2144394/?ito=vjs-link; (rebranded as an NHS challenge) DON'T RUSH DOCTORS CHALLENGE 🧑 ⚕ 🧑 ⚕ 🧑 ⚕ (medical edition) https://www.youtube.com/watch?v=kB_QbCt4I78

20 Turkish Airlines Don't Rush Challenge | #wewillsucceedtogether, https://www.youtube.com/watch?v=LoXt9Yp1Ck0

21 MILITARY DONT RUSH CHALLENGE W/ MY SISTERS IN ARMS, https://www.youtube.com/watch?v=iRSjlamXrUI

22 Best Don't rush challenge - South Africa, https://www.youtube.com/watch?v=oUoBoQnJ9jE; Don't Rush Challenge - Yemeni Queens, https://www.youtube.com/watch?v=3dk3RGR-x9s; #dontrushchallenge : Ghana 🇬🇭 girls edition, https://www.youtube.com/watch?v=uTLh_9zZaho

23 Young T & Bugsey - Don't Rush (Official #DontRushChallenge Compilation) ft. Headie One, https://www.youtube.com/watch?v=ILDpRrPTxkg

24 https://www.youtube.com/watch?v=ILDpRrPTxkg The song achieved commercial success, peaking within the top twenty of the UK Singles Chart, and received a nomination for the Brit Award for Song of the Year in 2021.

25 Young T & Bugsey X Rauw Alejandro - Don't Rush (Remix), https://www.youtube.com/watch?v=quKe_buY_Mo

26 Young T & Bugsey - Don't Rush (Lyric Video) ft. DaBaby, https://www.youtube.com/watch?v=2b3l_6Ke9iE

27 Isama, A. "The Real Reason the #DontRushChallenge Was Created". *Teen Vogue*, 7 April 2020, https://www.teenvogue.com/story/dont-rush-challenge-creator Twitter post from 22 March 2020 showing the first video can be seen here: https://twitter.com/lash_asolo/status/1241707263917723655

28 Isama, A. "The Real Reason the #DontRushChallenge Was Created"'; Boone, K. "Watch These Black Women Slay The 'Don't Rush Challenge'". *Essence*, 4 November 2020, https://www.essence.com/entertainment/dont-rush-challenge/

29 Herschmann, M. and Trotta, F., 2021. "Sonorous Windows in Times of Pandemic". *Revista Lusófona de Estudos Culturais/ Lusophone Journal of Cultural Studies*, 8(1), pp. 141–153.

30 Brock's critical technocultural discourse analysis (CTDA) analyses Black online presence across websites, platforms and services. See Brock Jr, A. *Distributed Blackness*.

31 Sobande, F., 2020. "Black Women's Digital Diaspora, Collectivity, and Resistance", in *The Digital Lives of Black Women in Britain*. (London: Palgrave Macmillan), pp. 101–129, p 102.

32 Ibid., pp. 103–104.

33 Brock Jr, A. *Distributed Blackness*, p. 214.

34 Mazibuko, M., 2023. "Semhle, Sbwl: Where Black Women Can Meet Grief During and Beyond a Pandemic", in Jordan-Zachery, J.S. (ed.), *Lavender Fields: Black Women Experiencing Fear, Agency, and Hope in the Time of COVID-19*. (Arizona: University of Arizona Press), pp. 200–201.

35 The lockdown period was effective for three weeks from March 27 and then extended to five weeks. Individuals could not leave

their homes except in exceptional circumstances or unless they were an essential worker. Public gatherings were also limited, travel restrictions were put in place, and schools were suspended. See Arndt, C. et al., 2020. "Covid-19 Lockdowns, Income Distribution, and Food Security: An Analysis for South Africa". *Global Food Security*, 26, p. 100410.

36 Mazibuko, M. "Semhle, Sbwl", p. 201.

37 Sobande, F. and Osei, K., 2020. "An African city: Black Women's Creativity, Pleasure, Diasporic (Dis)connections and Resistance Through Aesthetic and Media Practices And Scholarship". *Communication, Culture & Critique*, 13(2), pp. 204–221, p. 202.

38 Mazibuko, M. "Semhle, Sbwl", p. 194.

39 Nilson, H., 1998. "Technologies of the Self", in *Michel Foucault and the Games of Truth*. (London: Palgrave Macmillan), p. 97.

40 DeNora, T., 1999. "Music as a Technology of the Self". *Poetics*, 27(1), pp. 31–56.

41 Herschmann, M. and Trotta, F., 2021. "Sonorous Windows in Times of Pandemic". *Revista Lusófona de Estudos Culturais/ Lusophone Journal of Cultural Studies*, 8(1), pp. 141–153.

42 Ibid., p. 145.

43 Ibid., p. 146.

44 Ibid.

45 Ibid.

46 Long Covid or Post Covid syndrome is defined as: ongoing symptomatic COVID-19: signs and symptoms of COVID-19 from four to 12 weeks. post COVID-19 syndrome: signs and symptoms that develop during or after COVID-19 and continue for more than 12 weeks and are not explained by an alternative diagnosis.

See "What is Post-COVID syndrome/long COVID?", https://www. england.nhs.uk/coronavirus/post-covid-syndrome-long-covid/

47 McCarthy, J., 2021. *Who Will Pay Reparations on My Soul?: Essays*. (New York: Liveright Publishing), p. 245.

48 Military Dont Rush Challenge W/ My Sisters in Arms, https:// www.youtube.com/watch?v=iRSjlamXrUI

49 Female Police Officers Do The "Don't Rush" Challenge!, https://www.youtube.com/watch?v=dBNU-J0Ue8o

50 Bauman, Z., 2007. *Liquid Times: Living in an Age of Uncertainty*. (London: Polity Press), pp. 5–7.

51 See, for example, Fatsis, L., 2019. "Policing the Beats: The Criminalisation of UK Drill And Grime Music by the London Metropolitan Police". *The Sociological Review*, 67(6), pp. 1300–1316; Ilan, J., 2020. "Digital Street Culture Decoded: Why Criminalizing Drill Music Is Street Illiterate and Counterproductive". *The British Journal of Criminology*, 60(4), pp. 994–1013. Quinn, E., White, J. and Street, J., 2022. "Introduction to Special Issue: Prosecuting and Policing Rap". *Popular Music*, 41(4), pp. 419–426; Scott, C.D., 2020. "Policing Black Sound: Performing UK Grime and Rap Music Under Routinised Surveillance". *Soundings*, 75(75), pp. 55–65; White, J., 2017. "Controlling the Flow: How Urban Music Videos Allow Creative Scope and Permit Social Restriction". *Young*, 25(4), pp. 407–425.

Chapter 3: Musicking in Pandemic Time

1 Spence, K.M., 2021. "Caribbean Creatives and the Intelligent Economy".

2 See, for example, Elton John's one-hour benefit concert broadcast from his home, and John Legend playing live requests on Instagram. Reilly, N. "Elton John joined by Dave Grohl, Billie Joe Armstrong, Billie Eilish and more for live coronavirus relief concert". *NME*, 30 March 2020, https://www.nme.com/news/music/elton-john-joined-by-dave-grohl-billie-joe-armstrong-and-more-for-live-coronavirus-relief-concert-2637350

3 For example, in collaboration with T-Mobile, Justin Bieber livestreamed a New Year's Eve concert. T Mobile customers could watch for free, for others the ticket price was $25. See Paine, A. "Justin Bieber to perform first full-length concert since 2017 as New Year's Eve livestream". *Musicweek*, 30

December 2020, https://www.musicweek.com/digital/read/justin-bieber-to-perform-first-full-length-concert-since-2017-as-new-year-s-eve-livestream/082299

4   Small, C., 1998. *Musicking: The Meanings of Performing and Listening*. (Middletown: Wesleyan University Press).

5   Renihan, C. Brook, J. and Draisey-Collishaw, R., 2021 "Music Theatre 2.0: Re-Imagining Musicking in the Zoom Space". *Journal of Music, Health, and Wellbeing*, https://www.musichealthandwellbeing.co.uk/musickingthroughcovid19

6   Hesmondhalgh, D., 2013. *Why Music Matters*. (London: Wiley), p. 149.

7   Valverde, R.C., 2022. "Online Musicking for Humanity: The Role of Imagined Listening and the Moral Economies of Music Sharing on Social Media". *Popular Music*, 41(2), pp. 194–215.

8   In April 2022, Elon Musk acquired Twitter. The platform is now known as X, and the verification process is complex and ever-changing.

9   Baym, N.K. *Playing to the Crowd*, p. 156.

10 Valverde, R.C. "Online Musicking for Humanity".

11 Fairchild, C. and Marshall, P., 2019. "Music and Persona: An Introduction". *Persona Studies*, 5(1), pp. 1–16.

12 Mitchell, N., Thomas, K., Eagar, T. and Shi, Y. "Finding Space for Black Joy in Live Music During COVID-19". *Conference: ANZMAC (Australian and New Zealand Marketing Academy)*.

13 The *Verzuz* clash can be seen here: Bounty Killer Vs Beenie Man *Verzuz* Full Clash, https://www.youtube.com/watch?v=216ILslDOfs

14 Hope, D.P., 2006. *Inna Di Dancehall: Popular Culture and the Politics of Identity in Jamaica*. University of the West Indies Press.

15 Hope, D.P., 2006. *Inna Di Dancehall*.

16 Hope, D.P., 2006. *Inna Di Dancehall*.

17 Patten, H., 2022. *Reading Religion and Spirituality in Jamaican Reggae Dancehall Dance: Spirit Bodies Moving*. (London: Routledge), p. 2.

18 Cooper, C., 1994. "'Lyrical Gun": Metaphor and Role Play in Jamaican Dancehall Culture". *Massachusetts Review*, 35(3/4), pp. 429–447.

19 Stanley-Niaah, S. "Kingstons's Dancehall".

20 Bull, M. and Back, L. (eds), 2003. *Auditory Culture Reader*. (Oxford: Bloomsbury), p. 443.

21 Patten, H., 2022. *Reading religion and spirituality in Jamaican reggae dancehall dance: spirit bodies moving*. Routledge, Taylor & Francis Group. p. 3.

22 Gaunt, K. "'The Two O'Clock Vibe': Embodying the Jam of Musical Blackness In and Out of Its Everyday Context". *The Musical Quarterly,* 86(3), Fall 2002, pp. 372–397.

23 Stanley-Niaah, S., 2004. "Kingstons's Dancehall: A Story of Space and Celebration". *Space and Culture*, 7(1), pp. 102–118, p. 103.

24 In the 1950s and 1960s, anti-Black racism meant that the newly arrived West Indian community were not welcome in social clubs or pubs. "Blues parties" were put on as a way to socialise and hear music from home, and because partygoers paid an entrance fee, it was also a way to raise money. See White, J. *Urban Music and Entrepreneurship*, p. 32; and Palmer, L.A., 2011. "'Ladies a Your Time Now!' Erotic Politics, Lovers' Rock and Resistance in the UK". *African and Black Diaspora: An International Journal*, 4(2), pp. 177–192, p. 180.

25 Released in 1979, live recordings can be seen here: "JANET KAY Singing LIVE on 'Top of the Pops' 1979", https://www.youtube.com/watch?v=1dtYkuwukkI

26 "Small Axe: What Steve McQueen Got Right And Wrong About Lovers Rock". *The Conversation*, 30 November 2020, https://theconversation.com/small-axe-what-steve-mcqueen-got-right-and-wrong-about-lovers-rock-151068

27 Palmer, L.A. "'Ladies a Your Time Now!' Erotic Politics, Lovers' Rock and Resistance in the UK", p. 178.

28 Ibid., p. 178.

29 Dennis Bovell, guitarist, bass player and music producer, was a key figure in the early days of the lovers rock genre.

He wrote and produced "Silly Games" (sung by Janet Kay), which became a hit in the UK and across Europe. He produced albums by a wide variety of artists including the Thompson Twins, Bananarama and Madness. He also wrote the film score for 1980 film *Babylon*. Janet Kay is an actress and vocalist who had chart success with "Silly Games". Singer-songwriter Carroll Thompson is known as the "Queen of Lovers Rock". She has been a session singer for many artists including Michael Jackson, Stevie Wonder, Robbie Williams, Sting and Chaka Khan. Victor Romero Evans is a musician and an actor.

30 Just to point out that attendees were given the choice of writing their name, telephone number and contact email on a printed sheet, or downloading the Test and Trace app.

31 https://www.southbankcentre.co.uk/whats-on/gigs/dennis-bovell-presents-night-lovers-rock

32 Mitchell, N., Thomas, K., Eagar, T. and Shi, Y. "Finding Space for Black Joy in Live Music During COVID-19". *Conference: ANZMAC (Australian and New Zealand Marketing Academy)*, p. 218.

33 Platt, L., 2021. "COVID-19 and Ethnic Inequalities in England". *LSE Public Policy Review*, 1(4).

34 Mitchell, N., Thomas, K., Eagar, T. and Shi, Y., p. 218.

35 Hesmondhalgh, D. *Why Music Matters*, p. 168.

36 See, for example, Beenie Man Bounty Killer Go Wild When Rihanna Joins IG Live Battle, https://www.youtube.com/watch?v=-tCIjklY9aE

37 Hesmondhalgh, D. *Why Music Matters*, p. 2.

38 Ibid., p. 10.

39 Rose, T. *Black Noise*; White, J. *Urban Music and Entrepreneurship*.

40 Baym, N.K. *Playing to the Crowd*, p. 25.

41 Valverde, R.C. "Online Musicking for Humanity", p. 4.

42 Ibid., p. 6.

43 Ibid.

44 "Clubbing at Home: How Live Streaming Made DJ Sets More Inclusive". *The Conversation*, 27 November 2020, https://theconversation.com/clubbing-at-home-how-live-streaming-made-dj-sets-more-inclusive-149931

45 Howard, F. et al. "It's Turned Me from a Professional to a 'Bedroom DJ' Once Again'", p. 427.

46 Maloney, L., O'Neill, K. & Gray, J., 2021. "Alone Together: A Mixed-Methods Analysis of Spotify Listening During the COVID-19 Pandemic". *Journal of Music, Health, and Wellbeing*.

47 See Gross, S.A. and Musgrave, G., 2017. "Can Music Make You Sick (Part 2)? Qualitative Study and Recommendations". *Musictank*.

48 Recent research findings in a report from the ICO indicate that for music makers and music creators:
1. On-demand streaming now provides the main source of revenue for recorded music in the UK. Compared with the "pre-digital era", more rights holders and music creators are now competing for the diminished revenue from recorded music.
2. Half of musicians (47%) earned less than £10,000 from music in 2019.
3. Around 720 UK artists achieved one million UK streams per month — which the report suggests as a minimum threshold for making a sustainable living out of music.
"Between 2008–2019 revenues from streaming that performers and studio producers, composers and lyricists, and music publishers receive have declined. This is because there are increasing numbers of rights holders and music creators now competing for this revenue." See Hesmondhalgh, D., Osborne, R., Sun, H. and Barr, K., 2021. "Music creators' Earnings in the Digital Era". *Intellectual Property Office Research Paper* (forthcoming).

49 As a protest against racism and police brutality, millions of Instagram users shared black squares along with hashtags including #BlackOutTuesday and #BlackLivesMatter before pausing their social media content for the day. See Wellman,

M.L., 2022. "Black Squares for Black Lives? Performative Allyship as Credibility Maintenance for Social Media Influencers on Instagram". *Social Media+ Society*, 8(1), p. 2.

50 Hesmondhalgh, D. *Why Music Matters*, p. 170.

Chapter 4: Sonic Black Geographies

1   McKittrick, K., 2006. *Demonic Grounds: Black Women and the Cartographies of Struggle*. (Minneapolis: University of Minnesota Press), p. x.

2   Noxolo, P., 2020. "Introduction: Towards a Black British Geography?" *Transactions of the Institute of British Geographers*, 45(3), pp. 509–511, p. 509.

3   McKittrick, K. *Demonic Grounds*, p. xxi.

4   Some well-known crews included Roll Deep, Pay as U Go, East Connection, More Fire Crew, Heartless Crew and N.A.S.T.Y crew. See White, J. *Urban Music and Entrepreneurship: Beats, Rhymes and Young People's Enterprise.*

5   https://www.youtube.com/watch?v=LE7PWSRU5js — Romeo So Solid Crew, Wiley, Pay As U Go, HLC, Major Ace and Maxwell D Live at Alexander Palace 2002. During this live performance, Maxwell D, Romeo (from So Solid Crew), Major Ace and Wiley spit their bars over a garage/grime instrumental from DJ EZ, switching between a London and Jamaican dialect as they do so.

6   Gilroy, P., 1996. *The Black Atlantic*. (London: Verso).

7   Pirate radio in UK garage and grime scenes operated from an eclectic mix of venues, including council flats in tower blocks (see Mason, M., 2008. *The Pirate's Dilemma: How Hackers, Punk Capitalists, Graffiti Millionaires and Other Youth Movements are Remixing Our Culture and Changing Our World.* (London: Penguin), Wiley's mum's kitchen (see Wiley (2017) *Eskiboy*) and a treehouse on the A13 (rinsefm (2012) *18 Years of Rinse | 2009 : Marcus Nasty*, http://www.youtube.com/watch?v=xI8aA9ab_yg&feature=youtube_gdata_player)

8   See also White, J. "British Pirate Radio", https://
    artsandculture.google.com/story/british-pirate-radio-trench/
    KAUh6qSgSw1q-A?hl=en

9   Rose, T. *Black Noise*.

10 Ibid., p. 95.

11 James, M., 2020. *Sonic Intimacy: Reggae Sound Systems,
    Jungle Pirate Radio and Grime YouTube Music Videos*. (New
    York: Bloomsbury); White, J., 2021. "Growing Up Under
    the Influence: A Sonic Genealogy of Grime", in Henry, W.
    and Worley, M. (eds), *Narratives from Beyond the UK Reggae
    Bassline*. (Cham: Springer International Publishing).

12 Monrose, K., 2021. "Sound-Tapes and Soundscapes: Lo-Fi
    Cassette Recordings as Vectors of Cultural Transmission", in
    Henry, W. and Worley, M. (eds), *Narratives from Beyond the UK
    Reggae Bassline*.

13 Digital TV stations such as Channel U (later known as Channel
    AKA) which ran from February 2003 to June 2018. See White,
    J. *Urban Music and Entrepreneurship*.

14 The late Jamal Edwards was sixteen years old when he started
    SBTV in 2006 as an outlet to show the grime music videos that
    he created. Edwards turned SBTV into a global brand. Since
    then, a number of other channels have been established, such
    as Link up TV, an online youth channel founded in 2009 by
    seventeen-year-old Rashid Kasirye, and GRM Daily, an online
    music and news channel set up in 2009.

15 James, M., 2020. *Sonic Intimacy: Reggae Sound Systems, Jungle
    Pirate Radio and Grime YouTube Music Videos*. (New York:
    Bloomsbury).

16 Form 696 (ostensibly a risk assessment form but in reality a
    draconian measure that could result in a jail term of up to six
    months or a £20,000 fine) had been used to curtail or shut
    down live grime events. See Hancox, D. "Public enemy no 696".
    Guardian, 21 January 2009, https://www.theguardian.com/
    culture/2009/jan/21/police-form-696-garage-music

17 Fatsis, L. "Policing the Beats"; Stuart, F., 2021. *Ballad of the Bullet: Gangs, Drill Music, and the Power of Online Infamy*. (Princeton: Princeton University Press), p. 44.

18 Stuart, F. *Ballad of the Bullet*, p. 45.

19 White, J. *Urban Music and Entrepreneurship*; Fatsis, L., 2018. "Grime: Criminal Subculture or Public Counterculture? A Critical Investigation into the Criminalization of Black Musical Subcultures in the UK", *Crime, Media, Culture: An International Journal*.

20 Ilan, J. "Digital Street Culture Decoded".

21 Hancox, D., 2018. "The War Against Rap: Censoring Drill May Seem Radical But It's Not New". *Guardian*, 22 June 2018, https://www.theguardian.com/music/2018/jun/22/the-war-against-rap-censoring-drill-may-seem-radical-but-its-not-new; Thapar, C., 2019. "Don't Censor Drill Music, Listen to What It's Trying to Tell Us". *Guardian*, 6 February 2019, https://www.theguardian.com/commentisfree/2019/feb/06/dont-censor-drill-music-listen-skengdo-am; White, J., 2018. "Making Music Videos Is Not a Criminal Activity — No Matter What Genre". *The Conversation*, 22 June 2018, http://theconversation.com/making-music-videos-is-not-a-criminal-activity-no-matter-what-genre-97472

22 Fatsis, L. "Policing the Beats"; Ilan, J. "Digital Street Culture Decoded"; Pinkney, C. and Robinson-Edwards, S., 2018. "Gangs, Music and the Mediatisation of Crime: White, J. "Controlling the Flow".

23 Scott, C.D. "Policing Black Sound".

24 White, J., 2021. "Growing Up Under the Influence".

25 Fatsis, L. "Policing the Beats".

26 DGainz (2012). *Chief Keef - I Don't Like f/ Lil Reese | Shot by Dgainz*, https://www.youtube.com/watch?v=2WcRXJ4piHg

27 ManBetterKnow (2012). *I DON'T LIKE - JME JAMMER SKEPTA*, https://www.youtube.com/watch?v=Omlx8kdQF9g Calls in Barrington Levy's 1984 Dancehall anthem "Here I come" (Jet Star Music, 2018).

28 Ilan, J. "Digital Street Culture Decoded".

29 Stuart, F. *Ballad of the Bullet*, p. 3.

30 Pinkney, C. and Robinson-Edwards, S., 2018a. "Gangs, Music and the Mediatisation of Crime", p. 107

31 See, for example, Body — Russ Millions x Tion Wayne chart topping track which includes catchy dance moves, https://www.youtube.com/watch?v=gYPX5juKBvg

32 Stuart, F. *Ballad of the Bullet*.

33 Ibid., p. 3.

34 Ilan, J., 2020. "Digital Street Culture Decoded"; Thapar, C., 2021. *Cut Short: Why We're Failing Our Youth — And How to Fix It*. (London: Viking).

35 Lynes, A., Kelly, C. and Kelly, E., 2020. "THUG LIFE: Drill Music as a Periscope into Urban Violence in the Consumer Age". *The British Journal of Criminology*, 60(5), pp. 1201–1219.

36 Fatsis, L., 2019. "Policing the Beats".

37 Bramwell, R. and Butterworth, J., 2020. "Beyond the Street: The Institutional Life of Rap". *Popular Music*, 39(2), pp. 169–186.

38 Herlock, E., 2020. "How UK drill's filmmakers are driving its thriving scene". *DJMag.com*, https://djmag.com/longreads/how-uk-drill%E2%80%99s-filmmakers-are-driving-its-thriving-scene.

39 See, for example, Olusoga, D., 2016. *Black and British: A Forgotten History*. (London: Pan Macmillan).

40 Wacquant, L., 2007. *Urban Outcasts: A Comparative Sociology of Advanced Marginality*. (Malden: Polity).

41 Rose, T. *Black Noise*.

42 McKittrick, K. *Demonic Grounds*, p. xiv.

43 Reynolds, T., 2013. "'Them and Us': 'Black Neighbourhoods' as a Social Capital Resource among Black Youths Living in Inner-city London". *Urban Studies*, 50(3), pp. 484–498. doi: 10.1177/0042098012468892; White, J., 2019. "Growing Up in 'The Ends': Identity, Place and Belonging in an Urban East London Neighbourhood", in Habib, S. and Ward, M.R.M.

(eds), *Identities, Youth and Belonging: International Perspectives*. (Cham: Springer International Publishing), pp. 17–33.

44 Gunter, A., 2010. *Growing Up Bad? Black Youth, Road Culture and Badness in an East London Neighbourhood*. (London: Tufnell Press).

45 Earle, R., 2011. "Boys' Zone Stories: Perspectives from a Young Men's Prison". *Criminology and Criminal Justice*, 11(2), pp. 129–143, p. 134.

46 Ibid., p. 135.

47 Bakkali, Y., 2019. "Dying to Live: Youth Violence and the Munpain". *The Sociological Review*. SAGE Publications Ltd, 67(6), pp. 1317–1332.

48 Storrod, M.L. and Densley, J.A., 2017. "'Going Viral' and 'Going Country': The Expressive and Instrumental Activities of Street Gangs on Social Media". *Journal of Youth Studies*, 20(6), pp. 677–696. doi: 10.1080/13676261.2016.1260694.

49 Irwin-Rogers, K., Densley, J. and Pinkney, C., 2018. "Gang Violence and Social Media", in Ireland, J. L., Ireland, C.A., and Birch, P. (eds), *The Routledge International Handbook of Human Aggression*. (London: Routledge); Pinkney, C. and Robinson-Edwards, S. "Gangs, Music and the Mediatisation of Crime".

50 Bakkali, Y. "Dying to Live", p. 1327.

51 Reid, E., 2022 "'Trap Life': The Psychosocial Underpinnings of Street Crime in Inner-City London". *The British Journal of Criminology*, 60(4), pp. 994–1013.

52 White, J. "Growing Up in 'The Ends'".

53 Ellis-Petersen, H. "Police force entry to Stormzy's house after reports that he was burgling it". *Guardian*, 14 February 2017, https://www.theguardian.com/music/2017/feb/14/police-force-entry-to-stormzys-house-after-reports-that-he-was-burgling-it.

54 Fatsis, L. "Policing the Beats".

55 If a person is on licence (released before the full sentence ends) they can be taken back to prison if they break probation conditions.

56 Hinton, P., 2020. "Digga D threatened with recall to prison after joining Black Lives Matter protests". *Mixmag*, 16 June 2020, https://mixmag.net/read/digga-d-dutchavelli-black-lives-matter-protest-prison-news.

57 Rose, T. *Black* Noise, p. 19.

58 Gilroy, P., 2013. "'... We Got to Get Over Before We Go Under ...' Fragments for a History of Black Vernacular Neoliberalism". *New Formations*, (80/81).

59 Rose, T. *Black Noise*, p. 184.

60 White, J. and Ilan, J., 2021. "Ethnographer Soundclash: A UK Rap and Grime Story". *Riffs*, 5(2).

61 In Tottenham, north London, on 4 August 2011, Mark Duggan was shot dead by police. Protests soon turned to civil unrest, not only in London but also in other parts of the country.

62 https://www.ghetts.co.uk/home/

63 Identity Codes are used by UK police to describe assumed ethnic identity (for suspects or victims) — IC3 is the police code for Black. See National Police Chief Council Response to a Freedom of Information Request regarding IC codes, https://www.npcc.police.uk/2018%20FOI/IMORCC/182%2018%20NPCC%20Response%20Letter.pdf

64 Kano opens the song by calling in the first line of Jamaican reggae artist Sizzla's song "Just One Of Those Days (Dry Cry)" (2002). Sizzla's is a version of a Curtis Mayfield and the Impressions "Minstrel and Queen" (1962) released as "Queen Majesty" at various times by reggae artists such as the Techniques (1967) and Dennis Brown (1990). Kano Performs "Teardrops" | GRM Rated Awards 2020, https://www.youtube.com/watch?v=Onafw36BMIo&t=5s

65 The hostile environment has been in operation almost since the arrival of the post-war Commonwealth migrants. The "Windrush generation" refers to approximately 500,000 people who came to the UK from Caribbean countries between 1948 and 1971. Although adults were granted Indefinite Leave to Remain (ILR) in 1971, many were

children and had travelled on their parents' documents. In 2012, a further change to the law meant that without their own documents, this group of people could not continue to work or access services. In some cases, people were deported because they could not prove that they had a right to stay in the UK. See White, J., 2020. *Terraformed: Young Black Lives in the Inner City*. (London: Repeater). The British Library has a website that explores these issues in depth: https://www.bl.uk/windrush/themes/the-windrush-generation-scandal

66 "Three Rivers" https://www.youtube.com/watch?v=aZHfPt6u90A

67 "Cold" https://www.youtube.com/watch?v=wVyNovH0KFg

68 "New Noise: Kaash Page". *Wonderland Magazine*, 16 September 2020, https://www.wonderlandmagazine.com/2020/09/16/new-noise-kaash-paige/

69 TeeZandos - Need Focus - (2019) https://www.youtube.com/watch?v=FKGbSWL46GM

70 Herlock, E. "Hail Satan, TeeZandos Is Making Demonically Good Drill". *Vice*, 18 May 2020, https://www.vice.com/en/article/y3zzek/teezandos-drill-rapper-interview

71 TeeZandos - OT (Official Video), https://www.youtube.com/watch?v=AxEgQIi8XbU

72 Attali, J., 1985. *Noise: The Political Economy of Music*. (Minneapolis: University of Minnesota Press), p. 5.

73 Hall, S., 1992. "New Ethnicities", in Donald, J. and Rattansi, A. (eds), *Race, Culture and Difference*. (London: SAGE Publications).

74 McKittrick, K. *Demonic Grounds*, p. xx.

75 Gilroy, P. *The Black Atlantic*, p. 4.

76 Miles, C.J., 2023. *Vibe: The Sound and Feeling of Black Life in the American South*. (Jackson: University Press of Mississippi), p. 6.

77 Gayle, R., 2020. "Creative Futures of Black (British) Feminism in Austerity and Brexit Times". *Transactions of the Institute of British Geographers*, 45(3), pp. 525–528, p. 526.

78 Davies, S. "How UK rap became a multimillion-pound business". *Financial Times*, 9 August 2021, https://www.ft.com/content/58ecd23f-e1e7-4932-9d70-c57f1b170851

79 Rose, T. *Black Noise*, p. 6.

80 "Rap and Hip Hop soars in 2020 fuelled by streaming, new BPI insights show". *BPI*, https://www.bpi.co.uk/news-analysis/rap-and-hip-hop-soars-in-2020-fuelled-by-streaming-new-bpi-insights-show/

81 White, J. *Terraformed*.

Chapter 5: Modes of Entrepreneurship in Pandemic Time

1 "Arrive like you mean it" - Composed and produced by Kwame "Kz" Kwei-Armah Jnr, https://www.youtube.com/watch?v=tlRhEPnF9gQ

2 Remix Tion Wayne x Russ Millions - Body 2 ft Arrdee, 3x3E1 & ZT, Bugzy Malone, Fivio Foreign, Darkoo, Buni. Fivio Foreign is a rapper from Brooklyn in New York.

3 Dave - Funky Friday (ft. Fredo), https://www.youtube.com/watch?v=Pxns_n9q0f4

4 Spencer, K. "Stormzy becomes first Black British solo artist to headline Glastonbury Festival", *Sky News*, 29 June 2019, https://news.sky.com/story/its-only-the-beginning-stormzy-becomes-first-black-british-artist-to-headline-glastonbury-11751127

5 IKEA UK (2019) *IKEA – Silence The Critics - TV Advert 90 #WonderfulEveryday*. Available at https://www.youtube.com/watch?v=w0EKS2YfLc0

6 There is a great deal of academic scholarship on the importance of entrepreneurship. See, for example, Baumol, W.J., 1996. "Entrepreneurship: Productive, Unproductive and Destructive". *Journal of Business Venturing*, 11(1), pp. 3–22; Carland, H., Carland, J.W., Hoy, F. and Carland, J.A.C., 2002. "Who is an Entrepreneur? Is a Question Worth Asking". *Entrepreneurship: Critical Perspectives on Business*

and Management, 2, p. 178; Drucker, P. and Maciariello, J., 2014. *Innovation and Entrepreneurship*. (London: Routledge); Schumpeter, J.A., 2013. *Capitalism, Socialism and Democracy*. (London: Routledge); Shane, S. and Venkataraman, S., 2000. "The Promise of Entrepreneurship as a Field of Research". *Academy of Management Review*, 25(1), pp. 217–226.

7 Drucker, P. and Maciariello, J., 2014. *Innovation and Entrepreneurship*. (London: Routledge).

8 Baumol, W.J. "Entrepreneurship".

9 Schumpeter, J.A. *Capitalism, Socialism and Democracy*.

10 Shane, S. and Venkataraman, S. "The Promise of Entrepreneurship as a Field of Research".

11 See Kets de Vries, M.F., 1996. "The Anatomy of the Entrepreneur: Clinical Observations". *Human Relations*, 49(7), pp. 853–883 and Miller, D., 2015. "A Downside to the Entrepreneurial Personality?" *Entrepreneurship Theory and Practice*, 39(1), pp. 1–8.

12 Attali, J. *Noise*.

13 Musgrave, G. and Gross, S.A., 2020. *Can Music Make You Sick?*. (London: University of Westminster Press).

14 Wilson, J.A., 2011. "New-School Brand Creation and Creativity: Lessons from Hip Hop and the Global Branded Generation". *Journal of Brand Management*, 19, pp. 91–111.

15 Rose, T. *Black Noise*.

16 Sköld, D. and Rehn, A., 2007. "Makin' It, by Keeping It Real: Street Talk, Rap Music, and the Forgotten Entrepreneurship From 'the 'Hood'". *Group & Organization Management*, 32(1), pp. 50–78, p. 52.

17 Rose, T. *Black Noise*.

18 Drakopoulou Dodd, S. and Anderson, A.R., 2007. "Mumpsimus and the Mything of the Individualistic Entrepreneur". *International Small Business Journal*, 25(4), pp. 341–360; Thornton, P.H., Ribeiro-Soriano, D. and Urbano, D., 2011. "Socio-Cultural Factors and Entrepreneurial Activity: An Overview". *International Small Business Journal*, 29(2), pp. 105–118.

19 Quinn, E., 2004. *Nuthin' but a "G" Thang: The Culture and Commerce of Gangsta Rap.* (New York: Columbia University Press), p. 52.

20 White, J., 2018. "The Business of Grime". *CAMEo Research Institute for Cultural and Media.*

21 Drakopoulou Dodd, S. and Anderson, A. R. "Mumpsimus and the Mything of the Individualistic Entrepreneur".

22 UK producer 808Melo, a twenty-five-year-old from Ilford, on the outskirts of East London, came to the attention of Brooklyn drill rapper Pop Smoke via YouTube. Melo had provided production for a number of UK drill artists, including Headie One, and then went on to produce Pop Smoke's *Welcome to the Party* in 2019. As written in an interview with the *Face* in December 2019: "While browsing YouTube for beats last year, Pop Smoke happened to fall upon one called *Panic* by the then-unacquainted Melo [...]. Pop Smoke was mesmerised by the bristling drum work: as a youngster, he played African drums by hand in his local church, so he appreciates concussive thwacks when he hears them. 'When I heard his beat and them fucking drums — the way he dragged them drums — it stuck with me.'" Gannon, C. "Pop Smoke's London pilgrimage". *The Face*, 3 December 2019, https://theface.com/music/pop-smoke-hip-hop-drill-808melo-london

23 Maasø, A., 2018. "Music Streaming, Festivals, and the Eventization of Music". *Popular Music and Society*, 41(2), pp. 154–175.

24 Stuart, F. *Ballad of the Bullet,* p. 45.

25 Marshall, L., 2013. "The 360 Deal and the 'New' Music Industry". *European Journal of Cultural Studies*, 16(1), pp. 77–99.

26 Spence, K.M. "Caribbean Creatives and the Intelligent Economy".

27 Attali, J. *Noise*, p. 83.

28 Stuart, F. *Ballad of the Bullet.*

29 Attali, J. *Noise.*

30 Ibid., p. 8.

31 See, for example, Fatsis, L. "Grime"; Fatsis. L. "Policing the Beats"; Ilan, J. "Digital Street Culture Decoded"; Scott, C.D. "Policing Black Sound"; White, J. "Controlling the Flow".

32 The first Musicians' Census found that UK musicians' average annual income from music work is £20,700 — with 43% earning less than £14,000 a year from music. See Paine, A. "UK Musicians' Census reveals insights on earnings and career barriers". *Musicweek*, 11 September 2023, https://www.musicweek.com/talent/read/uk-musicians-census-reveals-insights-on-earnings-and-career-barriers/088479

33 White, J. *Urban Music and Entrepreneurship*.

34 Gilroy, P. "'… We Got to Get Over Before We Go Under …' Fragments for a History of Black Vernacular Neoliberalism", p. 34.

35 Quinn, E. *Nuthin' but a "G" Thang*.

36 Musgrave, G. and Gross, S.A., 2020. *Can Music Make You Sick?* University of Westminster Press.

37 Lockett, A., 2021. "What Is Black Twitter? A Rhetorical Criticism of Race, Dis/Information, and Social Media". *Race, Rhetoric, and Research Methods*, pp. 165–213, p. 167.

38 Brock Jr, A. *Distributed Blackness*, p. 80.

39 Ibid., p. 181.

40 Black Entertainment Television (BET) is a US Black music/entertainment channel: https://www.youtube.com/@BETNetworks/featured

41 See Addo, F. "How No Signal is Planning to Run Radio after Lockdown". *Dazed*, 4 September 2020, https://www.dazeddigital.com/music/article/50272/1/how-no-signal-is-planning-to-run-radio-after-lockdown

42 See also the BBC3 film: The Rise Of No Signal | Black Radio — Here To Stay, https://youtu.be/1XD_Xlaag6E?si=sHT4onKhMhHwsrCP

43 "'Whether it be R&B, soca, drill or dancehall,' says Joseph, also known as VI, who is head of programming at the station, 'we wanted to represent the black diaspora as a whole. That's

what we listen to at home or out in the clubs.'" Ekpoudom, A. "'We want people to feel they have a home': No Signal, black Britain's new radio station". *Guardian*, 16 June 2020, https://www.theguardian.com/music/2020/jun/16/we-want-people-to-feel-they-have-a-home-no-signal-black-britains-new-radio-station

44   The London Borough of Newham was one of the densely populated, poor and ethnically diverse areas most affected by Covid-19 in the early days of the pandemic. In May 2020, the Office for National Statistics reported:
"When adjusting for size and age structure of the population, there were 36.2 deaths involving COVID-19 per 100,000 people in England and Wales [...]. The local authorities with the highest age-standardised mortality rates for deaths involving COVID-19 were all London Boroughs; Newham had the highest age-standardised rate with 144.3 deaths per 100,000 population". Caul, S., 2020. "Deaths involving COVID-19 by local area and socioeconomic deprivation: deaths occurring between 1 March and 17 April 2020". *Office for National Statistics*, 1.
See also Raval, A. "Inside the 'Covid Triangle': A catastrophe years in the making". *Financial Times*, 5 March 2021, https://www.ft.com/content/0e63541a-8b6d-4bec-8b59-b391bf44a492

45   https://www.youtube.com/@kano/videos

46   https://www.gofundme.com/f/NewhamTalks
"Each episode featured Kano and a different Newham native — Grime MCs; Ghetts, D Double E, Footsie, *GRM Daily* founder Posty, Commonwealth 400 m champion Christine Ohuruogu, actor Idris Elba, author Joy White, vegan chef King Cook and former footballer Chris Hughton — discussing growing up in the borough, the road to success, lessons learned along the way and more". Beneficiary organisations were The Renewal Programme, Caritas House and Bonny Downs Community Association.

47 Some examples here from *GRM Daily*, *Newham Recorder* and *DJ Mag*: https://grmdaily.com/posts/?s=newham+talks https://www.newhamrecorder.co.uk/news/21421776.east-ham-rapper-kano-homegrown-guest-stars-team-video-series-aid-newham-charities/ https://djmag.com/news/kano-launches-talk-series-and-fundraiser-newham-community-renewal-programme

48 White, J. *Terraformed*.

49 Care Collective, the, 2020. *The Care Manifesto: The Politics of Interdependence: The Politics of Compassion*. (London: Verso Books), pp. 95–97.

50 Renihan, C. Brook, J. and Draisey-Collishaw, R. "Music Theatre 2.0", pp. 5–6.

51 Ilan, J. "Digital Street Culture Decoded".

52 Irwin-Rogers, K., Densley, J. and Pinkney, C. "Gang Violence and Social Media"; Pinkney, C. and Robinson-Edwards, S. "Gangs, Music and the Mediatisation of Crime".

53 Ilan, J. "Digital Street Culture Decoded".

54 Amnesty UK, 2018. *Trapped in the Matrix: Secrecy, stigma, and bias in the Met's Gangs Database*. (Amnesty UK).

55 Ruth Eikhof, D. and Warhurst, C., 2013. "The promised land? Why social inequalities are systemic in the creative industries". *Employee Relations*, 35(5), pp. 495–508.

56 Quinn, E., 2004. *Nuthin' but a "G" Thang: The Culture and Commerce of Gangsta Rap*; Rose, T. *Black Noise*.

57 Fatsis, L. "Policing the Beats"; Ilan, J., 2020. "Digital Street Culture Decoded"; White, J. "Controlling the Flow"; White, J. *Urban Music and Entrepreneurship*; White, J. *Terraformed*.

58 Elliott, L. "World's 10 richest men see their wealth double during Covid pandemic". *Guardian*, 17 January 2022, https://www.theguardian.com/business/2022/jan/17/world-10-richest-men-see-their-wealth-double-during-covid-pandemic.

59 Haynes, J. and Marshall, L., 2018. "Reluctant Entrepreneurs: Musicians and Entrepreneurship in the 'New' Music Industry". *The British Journal of Sociology*, 69(2), pp. 459–482, p. 461.

60   Baym, N.K. *Playing to the Crowd.*
61   Musgrave, G. and Gross, S.A., *Can Music Make You Sick?*, p. 46.
62   Ibid., p. 44.
63   Spence, K.M., 2021. "Caribbean Creatives and the Intelligent Economy".

Conclusion: It's Not Over Yet...

1   https://covid19.public-inquiry.uk/every-story-matters/.
2   The Centre for Social Justice is a right-wing think-tank founded by Iain Duncan Smith. Their report *Two Nations: The State of Poverty in the UK* looked at the challenges faced by the most deprived communities against the backdrop of Covid-19.
3   Brooks, S.K. et al., 2020. "The psychological impact of quarantine and how to reduce it: Rapid review of the evidence". *The Lancet*, 395(10227), pp. 912–920.
4   Hylland, O.M., 2022. "Tales of temporary disruption: Digital adaptations in the first 100 days of the cultural Covid lockdown". *Poetics*, 90(101602).
5   Brook, O., O'Brien, D. and Taylor, M., 2020. *Culture Is Bad for You.* (Manchester: Manchester University Press), p. 649.
6   Hesmondhalgh, D. *Why Music Matters.*
7   Davies, W., Jai Dutta, S. and Taylor, N. *Unprecedented?*
8   Build Back Fairer: The COVID-19 Marmot Review, https://www.health.org.uk/publications/build-back-fairer-the-covid-19-marmot-review
9   Bauman, Z. *Liquid Times*, p. 2.
10   Gilroy, P. "Vexed History", p. 27.
11   Ibid., p. 28.
12   Hesmondhalgh, D. and Baker, S., 2013. *Creative labour: Media work in three cultural industries.* (Routledge). Cited in Baym, N.K. *Playing to the Crowd*, p. 25.
13   Baym, N.K. *Playing to the Crowd*, p. 26.
14   Miles, C.J., 2023. *Vibe: The Sound and Feeling of Black Life in the American South.* (Jackson: University Press of Mississippi), p. 22.

15 http://www.youtube.com/@xconversation

16 The UK has a prison population of approximately eighty-seven
    thousand — one of the highest in Europe. https://www.gov.
    uk/government/publications/prison-population-figures-2024.
    Many prisoners in England and Wales are locked in their
    cells for up to twenty-three hours each day. See Bychawski,
    A. "Prisoners still being locked up for 23 hours a day despite
    record self-harm". *openDemocracy*, 20 February 2023, https://
    www.opendemocracy.net/en/prisons-hmp-exeter-bullingdon-
    forest-bank-wakefield-time-in-cell/

17 Scorcher (Tayó Grant Jarrett) a north London grime
    MC, songwriter and actor, was the first guest interview
    shown over two episodes: https://www.youtube.com/
    watch?v=ykCOECTVAMM - SCORCHER - XCONVERSATION
    - SCORCHING A PATH - Ep 1; https://www.youtube.com/
    watch?v=WpCiiA8J4mQ - SCORCHER - XCONVERSATION -
    SCORCHING A PATH pt2

18 https://healingjusticeldn.org/

19 https://www.maiagroup.co/about-us

ACKNOWLEDGEMENTS

Completing this book took far longer than expected, so first things first, I must thank Tariq Goddard for agreeing to publish and to all at Repeater for their patience and efforts in bringing it into being. I need to also shout out the following people whose contributions helped me to pull this into some sort of shape: Jacqueline White and Mark Kane, my colleagues at the University of Bedfordshire, who bravely read the very early, barely formed drafts of the initial chapters; Kim-Marie Spence, who helped me to fine-tune my thinking on Jamaica's significance in the global creative industries; Lisa Amanda Palmer for insightful questions that helped to define the content and direction of the work; Jonathan Ilan and Ebony Reid for reading and discussing later versions and providing valuable comments on the framing and structure; and Blossom Lewis and Yvonne Robinson for listening to the audio recordings and offering a much-needed reader's perspective. Last, and certainly not least, my daughter Karis, who kept an elbow at my back and encouraged me to continue with the task of starting and finishing this book. If I have left anyone out, I apologise, but know that I appreciate everyone, named or otherwise, for pouring into me so that I could get it finished. Any errors or omissions are all mine, but I would not have got here without the village. Thank you.

Repeater Books

is dedicated to the creation of a new reality. The landscape of twenty-first-century arts and letters is faded and inert, riven by fashionable cynicism, egotistical self-reference and a nostalgia for the recent past. Repeater intends to add its voice to those movements that wish to enter history and assert control over its currents, gathering together scattered and isolated voices with those who have already called for an escape from Capitalist Realism. Our desire is to publish in every sphere and genre, combining vigorous dissent and a pragmatic willingness to succeed where messianic abstraction and quiescent co-option have stalled: abstention is not an option: we are alive and we don't agree.